The Catholic Red Pill

By James DePrisco

"The Catholic Redpill" by James A. DePrisco Copyright 2019. All Rights Reserved

Cover Girl by M.J. Rodriquez Copyright 2019. Used with permission.

Cover Art by Jimencio Arte Copyright 2019. Used with permission.

If you would like to hire the cover girl for a shoot, you can contact Mary Jo at photos_mjrodriquez@yahoo.com. She is used to working on projects remotely.

If you would like to contact the artist (including work with green screens), you can contact him at Jimencio @Jimencio Arte or through Mary Jo.

This book is dedicated to the semi colon; an underutilized but most excellent punctuation mark. In this book it may be over utilized, but that is part of the strategy for bringing it back.

Introduction

Ever since your mamma sat your diapered ass in front of the TV to watch Sesame Street, you have been undergoing programming into a sick culture based on leftism, feminism, depravity, and even atheism. This programming was reinforced throughout your life: in your schooling, in the music you hear, the movies you watch, the TV you pollute your brain with, the commercials – it's everywhere, demoralizing you and keeping you from what you are ordered to be: a man.

The result? Taken to the extreme you have been reduced to a hand wringing whiner with an excuse in every pocket. Women despise you even though you follow your programming and try to please them. You have no mechanical skills and break out into a sweat just thinking about manual work. You've never shot a gun or gone fishing, and you've never worshiped at the iron temple of the weight pile. You don't even know a darn thing about what I just wrote.

Hopefully it has not taken you down this far in the pit, but today it would not surprise me. Even if you are not as bad as that, all of us, including me, have undergone some degree of the demoralization process, a process that is the core of something called Cultural Marxism. But there is hope. As I wrote, you are ordered to be a man. No matter how far gone you are, there is always a way back home. You are naturally ordered to manful living, and therein lies your hope.

This book is your answer. Read it. Understand it. Follow it. And after you have fully digested it, refer to it weekly to tune up areas that need work.

You my friend are taking the red pill, The Catholic Red Pill. Remember, there is no going back once you have taken the Red Pill, but I promise you, you would never want to.

Oh, I almost forgot. Welcome ladies. A book about men written for men? Of course their curious little brains can't resist. Lads, you have a lot to learn, so let's begin.

Section 1: Frame

The Pedigree of the Catholic Red Pill

We have to start at a beginning. I don't know precisely what "the" beginning is, perhaps Adam and Eve, but I can give you "a" beginning.

Our story starts with Gramsci, the true father of Cultural Marxism. Faced with the continuous defeat of the glorious communist revolution, he identified cultural hegemony, in his particular "Italian" case the overriding power of the Catholic Church in Italy, which communism could not defeat directly. The only answer was weakening, if not destroying the Church: a "march through the institutions". Ultimately this led to communist infiltration into the Church and Vatican II; but that is not the topic of this book.

After Gramsci the next important character was Gyorgy Lukacs. Faced with another communist defeat in Catholic Hungary he fled to Germany to form his Frankfurt School with Max Horkheimer, Theodor W. Adorno, Erich Fromm, and Herbert Marcuse wherein they formalized Cultural Marxism with their Critical Theory. The Frankfurt School fled to the USA after the rise of Hitler and brought Critical Theory with them. This Frankfurt School began the formal attack on the culture of Christendom.

At some point the KGB got involved (Bella Dodd was active in the 30's and 40's infiltrating homosexuals into seminaries) with their own related program called demoralization. All of this reached its climax with Alinsky and the destruction of Christian culture in the West. As former KGB agent Yuri Bezmenov has stated the process of demoralization has reached such an advanced state in the USA that the KGB no longer had to be involved: "You are doing it to yourselves now.". He said this back in the 80's before the fall of the Soviet Union.

This then traces the collapse. It was a deliberate operation carried out by the Marxists in order to destroy the culture of the West and the Catholic Church in particular, and it has been all but a complete success. This is the reason why you see the insanity around you, especially when you compare it to the culture seen in older movies on Netflix or Youtube; you get the feeling that the past United States was an alien society.

But the story did not end there. Out of this catastrophe a reaction has sprung up and it is fighting back. It started innocently enough, and for the basest of reasons. Brainwashed men utilized the "inclusion" and feminism that they were taught in an effort to pick up women for fornication. Their results were horrible. A small group of men started experimenting with techniques, basically doing the exact opposite of what they were programmed to do and realized promising results. An internet forum called "So Suave" was a major gathering place for men experimenting with these techniques during the early years. Men were fornicating with different women every weekend and sharing their techniques. While the goals and some of the methods were sinful, the important point was that men were realizing that they had been lied to. This group of men are called the Pick Up Artists, also known as PUA's and what they do is commonly referred to as Game. And they have spread in popularity due to the internet and number in the thousands, maybe even over a million.

During the development of PUA a separate phenomenon was going on. Men had abandoned TV and retreated to video games, especially online games where they could form online friendships with other men using voice communications through head sets. These were the gamers and the games they played were violent and filled with masculine themes. The Cultural Marxists realized the threat this posed to their goals, since gaming, which they did not control, was replacing TV; and through a coordinated effort (confirmed by leaked documents discovered by hackers) tried to take over gaming and use it as a vector to inject their demoralization. I want to stress this point: this is not conspiracy theory, the leaked plans of the cultural marxists, obtained by hackers, details a coordinated effort to take over video games ("the death of gamers" incident).

The gamers fought back in what soon became known as #GamerGate – and won. #GamerGate was another lesson taught to men: the coordinated effort to feminize them was revealed and methods for defeating the Cultural Marxists were developed, e.g. meme wars, trolling, and a battle slogan: "WE. DON'T. CARE.".

Back in the PUA camp a subset of men started to realize something. "Game" involved presenting highly masculine traits to women, who responded with fornication. This group of men began to change their perception about Game; it was not merely a way to seduce women for free sex, it was instead the way to live your life -- a masculine life that all men are ordered to live. This group became known as the Manosphere and in particular TradCons. A smaller subset (definitely not Trad Catholic) viewed the culture as so diseased that it was best to avoid women all together, but at a minimum to avoid any committed relationships. This group is known as MGTOW (Men Going Their Own Way) and are not really relevant to this book.

All of these various threads combined into what is today called The Red Pill. The political wing is known as the Alt-Right and got Donald Trump elected as President. This movement is now world wide and especially popular in the USA, the UK, and Australia, though there are respectably sized groups in Germany and other countries as well. Note at the time that I am writing this book the Marxists have successfully coopted the term Alt-Right to mean "neo-nazi", so that term is being replaced by "New Right".

Taken as a whole the Red Pill is a huge improvement over the feminized culture, and a Catholic man can benefit from reading some of the Red Pill blogs and watching some of the Red Pill videos. The morality in it is a big problem though. In some groups (not all) men are told to watch porn, masturbate, and fornicate with women. Atheism is present in some wings and evolutionary beliefs are widespread. God is absent. Furthermore it has no philosophy unless you count materialism (evolution) as a philosophy. It is mainly empirical: men improve their lives by rejecting effeminacy and embracing masculinity, so keep being masculine. In short it abandons unnatural sin for natural sin (though in a few cases with Trad Cons chastity is promoted). Note that secular Western men had rediscovered what was once common knowledge: a life of Catholic Virtue (however distorted).

Catholics need something better then these empirical observations. They won't find it in the Novus Ordo where oftentimes they are preached to by a homosexual priest. Many Trad Chapels are only a little better as they have overreacted and taken up a neo-Manicheanism, i.e. the view that the material world is not important. For example, in many Trad high schools math stops at Algebra II.

And thus we have arrived at this book, which will take the empiricism of the Red Pill along with lessons from our Grandfathers, and combine this with Catholic morality, virtue, and philosophy resulting in The Catholic Red Pill. This is your manual to live your life as you have been ordered to live it by God. You will relearn something which was once common knowledge, otherwise known as Catholic virtue. This book will help you defeat our enemies on the left -- the Cultural Marxists and feminists who want to rob you of your masculinity, and our enemies on the Right -- those Catholics who have given in to overreaction and want you to abandon your State in Life to live as a man in the material world, neglecting the forgotten virtue: Magnanimity.

Let us continue.

Defining Frame

The most important concept for you to learn is called Frame. Unfortunately the terminology surrounding it can be confusing and used in different ways. I'll give you an example with this true statement: "A man with strong frame easily reframes.".

Let's break it down, and I'll give you my definition of Frame (there are others). First we can divide it into the verb and the noun. The verb is easy, and we will more-or-less discard it. The verb is "to frame" or "to reframe". To Frame means to create a mindset or how you think about something. To Reframe means to change your mindset, or someone else's mindset. This definition will only play a minor role in this book.

And now the noun. To put it simply, Frame is who you are. So if you have a strong frame, then you are a strong and masculine man. If your frame is weak, then you are weak -- given to emotionalism, whining, and pouting. A man with strong frame readily provides value to others. A man with weak frame sucks value from others. (Read those last two sentences 20 times). If you are familiar with Red Pill terminology, the man with strong frame is the extrovert Alpha or the introvert Sigma, while the man with weak frame is the extrovert Gamma or the introvert Omega. The extrovert Beta and introvert Delta fall somewhere in between.

Just as a picture frame has four sides, your frame is composed of four sides. You will learn about each side and work on strengthening each one. As your frame strengthens, you will strengthen and become more masculine. As an added benefit strong frame is catnip to the ladies. Paraphrasing the Dead Poet Society in describing the benefits of poetry, I'll say that one of the uses of strong frame is to woo women, either your future girlfriend or even your wife.

This then is the overview. As I walk you through each side of Frame and what you need to do to develop and strengthen it, you will gain a deeper understanding of what Frame is, and especially what constitutes Strong Frame.

Side One: Body

The first side of your frame is your body, its health and your appearance. This side of frame includes sleep, addiction breaking, physical strength, good nutrition, a proper percent body fat, aerobic capacity, hygiene, appearance (clothing and hair), and fighting ability.

Sleep: Most likely after reading the first few pages of this book, you are getting motivated. You suspect that you are holding gold in your hands. You are pumped, and some of you will even read this whole book in one sitting. Let that sink in, because I need to really stress this. What is the first actionable item (and there will be many) that you have come across? What takes the pride of place? SLEEP. For if you are unwilling to make some changes and get control of your sleep schedule, I'm sorry, but you have wasted your money. Don't waste anymore time reading this book and throw it in the trash. If you don't get your sleep, you will not improve.

You know what you have to do, but I'll give you some key points:

1. As important as the amount of sleep, keeping a regular sleep schedule is critical. This means going to bed every night at about the same time, and getting up in the morning at the same time. Now if you are 18, you are pretty much screwed. You work or go to school during the week, getting up early until Friday night comes. You'll stay up to 3 a.m. with your buddies and crash on Saturday.

Now this book has to be realistic (Cardinal Virtue of Prudence), so we have to deal with this. My advise is to make Friday night party night or a night of swing dancing, then use Saturday and Saturday night as a more laid back time with your buddies. Saturdays are a good day to go camping, fishing, or hunting. If you want some leisure for Saturday night, coordinate that around grilling out. Put some steaks, burgers, or chicken on the grill, drink a few beers, and socialize. You'll still go to bed later than normal, but it is easier to "call it a night" and hit the pillow before midnight. Do what you can and keep the goal of regular sleep in front of you.

2. Sleep cycles: The human brain goes through roughly 1 -1/2 hour sleep cycles. If your alarm clock goes off in the middle of a cycle you will feel like you were run over by a truck when you wake up. Has this ever happened to you: you pop awake at 5 a.m. feeling really good on one day, vs. waking up at 7 a.m. and feeling like crap on another? The sleep cycle phenomenon explains this. Using sleep cycles, I present to you the following guidelines (adding 40 minutes for prep time, and time to fall asleep):

a. 6 hours, 40 minutes. Bare minimum. Once per week is barely acceptable. This gives you 20 minutes to brush your teeth and say your prayers, and 20 minutes to fall asleep.

b. 8 hours, 10 minutes. Maintenance sleep. This should be the bulk of your schedule.

c. 9 hours, 40 minutes. Recovery sleep. Target this amount if you are sleep deprived. You can add 1-1/2 hour cycles as needed to recover from any sleep deprivation. Hopefully this is rare.

3. The Pious Catholic: If you are saying 15 decade rosaries and multiple litanies every night, this could be a problem. If this is what you do before bedtime, you might build up a dread of going to bed since you are facing an hour and a half torture session. Be ruthless in your self assessment. If you are sleep deprived and feel like crap, eliminate your crazy prayer schedule for one month and fall back on the Catholic

requirements: A 30 second morning offering in the morning, and a 30 second Act of Contrition at night. This is all the Church requires, so lose the spiritual pride. Do this for a month with the assumption you are working on regaining your rest. After that period of time, add back prayers that are meaningful and that comport to your State in Life. But doing evil, e.g. depriving yourself of sleep, in order to pray is NOT pious. Another suggestion is to move some of your prayers to your lunch break.

4. Caffeine: Simple. No caffeine after 2 p.m. You should also have a goal to eliminate all caffeine after you have recovered a rested State. Also note that drinking caffeine in the morning at work will leave you feeling washed out when you get home in the evening if you cut it off at a reasonable time – another reason to quit.

<u>Addictions:</u> There are some common addictions that hold you back. In discussing this topic it is important to understand a system in your brain called the dopaminergic system. When you accomplish a goal, your brain releases some dopamine that makes you feel good. For example, if you change the oil on your car, upon completion you will get a slight dopamine hit. With that in mind, now consider someone doing a line of coke, which directly stimulates the brain's dopamine center. Note that after a short while you will build up a tolerance to these large doses of cocaine induced dopamine. Going forward working on your car provides such a tiny amount of dopamine that you no longer feel the reward of satisfaction for completing a task. Can you understand why drug use leads to junkies lying in the gutter? Now here is the scary part: imagine the dump of dopamine you receive when you defeat the super villain in a video game. Or imagine the constant hits of dopamine the ladies get whenever they hear an alert that they have received a new text. Do you now understand why a lot of women are

addicted to incessant texting? And here in lies the problem: with addictions you destroy your dopamine system and completing productive tasks no longer FEELS rewarding. This is a big problem. On the plus side removing the artificial dopamine hits will restore your system to normal.

Here are the main addictions you need to overcome if they control you:

1. Electronic addictions. These include video games, computer games, social media, binge watching Youtube, Netflix, and TV. First the easy one. Cancel the cable and quit watching TV. I've heard a priest describe it as an open sewer running straight into your house. Cut it off today.

As far as the rest, the first attempt is to establish control. Make it your rule that these activities shall not interfere with your bedtime. If you can't do that, most likely you will have to go cold turkey. If it is 3 a.m. and you look down and there is a game controller in your hand, you have a problem. There is one last thing to try before you go cold turkey.

Electronics fast. Pick 3 days a week where you "fast" from electronics. No cheating, no excuses. Through this fasting you may build up the will power to regain control and respect your bedtime. This fasting means absolutely no electronic activities, e.g. substituting a computer game for a video game breaks the fast. One of the days should be Sunday as you get the benefit of a good night sleep for Monday morning (school or work). Or you could have the fast start Sunday at 5 p.m. because Sunday is traditionally a leisure day. As a trick you can set an alarm or a reminder on your phone to start a Sunday fast at 5 p.m. If you can't successfully fast for 3 days a week, then it must be cold turkey. Cut it off for a month, and then maybe try to reintroduce it where you have control.

Furthermore evaluate if an electronics addiction is interfering with your life. Are you keeping up with your chores? Do you have a social life? How often do you do outdoor activities like going fishing with your buddies?

Besides entertainment, there is social media. I personally think Facebook is gay, so there's that also. Included in this is incessant texting, which is gay. Knock it off. Finally we have forums and comment sections. Keep those under control -- social media should be used as a tool, if at all.

On a personal note, my weakness is Youtube binge watching and Netflix documentaries. I admit it, I'm an addict and have had to go cold turkey. Let's face it, there is a lot of value on Youtube and on the Netflix documentaries, but I'm an addict, so I've cut them off completely.

Note I'm not against using electronics for some leisure. That is fine. However when you lose control, and this usually shows up as sleep deprivation and "falling behind", you need to own your addiction and kill it.

2. Caffeine. Caffeine makes you groggy in the morning. I'm a caffeine addict, however I found that if I cut off the caffeine at 2 p.m., usage is tolerable, though I do feel "washed up" at the end of work because I'm coming off the caffeine high. My main problem is that I love the taste of a good cup of black coffee. However, if it doesn't interfere with your sleep, this is minor.

To quit, switch to a tasty diet soda like Coke Zero and work yourself off over 2 weeks. This avoids the caffeine headache. If you screw up and get a headache, pop 2 Advil and drink some Coke Zero and the headache quickly goes away. Wean off slowly over 2 weeks and you should be good.

3. Nicotine. I write this while cranking a dip of Copenhagen (pouches) right now. Nicotine is a stimulant and can keep you up at night. There are also the health problems that go along with it. Luckily the patch works. Here's a system I used successfully in the past, and will use again:
a. Use a quality patch like Nicotrol. Habitrol is marginally acceptable.
b. 21 m.g. for 7 days. If you are really addicted, then go 14 days.
c. 14 m.g. for 14 days.
d. 10 m.g. for 7 days. Cut the 21 m.g. patch in half, ignore any warnings on the label, it is a scam.
e. 7 m.g. for 7 days.
f. 3.5 m.g. for 7 days. Again, cut the 7 m.g. in half.
g. After that, it is easy to quit. I recommend starting this program on a low stress weekend. Start off the morning with your morning shower dip or your morning cigarette, then go on the patch. Throw out all tobacco products.
i. One important warning. DO NOT SLEEP WITH THE PATCH. It will give you some crazy dreams, at least with the higher dose patches. I screwed up one time and had an interesting dream talking to people with blood dripping out of their eyes. This is a well documented phenomenon called "vivid dreams".

4. Drugs or alcohol. Dry out and get off that stuff. For alcohol, switch to beer. It will make you fat and it is hard to drink a lot of it. Seems like the easy way off. Work your way off slowly.

<u>Physical Strength:</u> Probably the most important thing you can do after taking the Red Pill and working on your sleep is to worship at the iron temple of the weight pile. This means working out with a buddy with free weights -- pumping iron. I used to work out at a gym that had a sign on the wall which read: "No machines, no chrome, no fags, just iron". Pumping

iron gives you a "V" shaped body that the ladies are crazy for, and it blasts up the testosterone. It is critical to lift.

Now let's be reasonable. Suppose you can't find a work out buddy, which means no one to spot you on the bench press. In that case, then yes buy/use a machine that allows you to do bench presses, etc... The important goal is to build up your muscles. However, do try to get a spotter, or if you have the money hire a trainer at the gym who can spot you. Now if you are forced to go the machine route, then at least buy a set of dumb bells, 10-40 lb. range to start out, and a 25 lb. curl bar with some plates. You'll also need a pull-up rack that allows you to do pull ups. In the next section, I'll give advise to the absolute beginner. It is in italics, so if you already have gym experience, skip this section.

I want to take the case of the bean pole who has zero muscles and has never lifted. I advise you to build up some strength before hitting the gym. Your goal is to be able to crank out 2 sets of 20 pushups, 2 sets of 20 crunches, and 2 sets of 6 pull ups. Let me walk you through it.

On pushups, find out what you can do right now. Maybe you can do 8 pushups. Do those 3 nights in a row, with a day off to break it up. So maybe you take Wednesday and Saturday off. Add 2 pushups every week until you build up to 2 sets of 20. At that point you'll be able to get started at the gym.

Crunches are similar to sit ups. Go to your couch and lie in front of it on the floor, with your feet on the couch and your butt almost touching the edge of the couch so you are kind of crunched up. Put your hands behind your head with your fingers interlocked and do "sit ups". Build up to 2 sets of 20.

On pull ups, you will have to go and buy a pull up frame. You probably can't do one pull up, so put a chair under the frame and cheat with your feet. Start off doing 2 sets of 6, using the chair and your feet to cheat it. Once you touch the back of your neck, don't use your feet at all and try to slowly lower yourself back down. Over time, use your legs less and less. Maybe you can crank out 2 good pull ups, then start cheating for the last 4. Keep going until you can do 6 pull ups. Note you should take a wide grip, wider than your shoulders, and touch the back of your neck. The wider grip concentrates the work out on your back.

Now my advise for the gym. There are many "systems" that you can follow, and I don't claim mine is the best one, but it has worked for me. Sure if you are working out with a trainer and he has what he claims is a better system (and he's ripped), go ahead and follow it. My system works and if you and your buddy are just getting started, it will give you results you'll like. I'm talking about the old school 10-8-6, adding 10 pounds to each set. I used it when I wrestled in college and could bench twice my body weight. I use it today and I'm cut, so it will work for you. One important point, start lighter than you think you can do and concentrate on precise form starting out. Here is a good work out program, and note all use a 10-8-6 with 5 lbs. added to each side between reps:

(Monday, Thursday)

Bench Press: The king of the weight pile. This is done "on the bench" on your back. You use a 45 lb. bar and stack plates on either end. If you are starting out, you might start with a 25 lb. plate on either side, so you would do 10 reps of 95 lbs., 8 reps of 105 lbs., then move up to 35 lb. plates on each side for 6 reps of 115 lbs. Your buddy does his reps between yours. This exercise builds up your chest, front shoulder, and triceps (back of upper arm). A good first target to work towards is to start out near your body weight for your first set. You can work even higher, but at this point you will have bulked up and have some definition.

Butterflys: This is done on your back with dumb bells. To teach the proper form, we'd tell people to "hug the tree". The starting position is with the dumb bells over your chest and your arms forming a big circle like you are hugging a tree. The dumb bells are touching such that the corresponding fingers on each hand are almost touching. You then lower the dumb bells to the side of you, but you make sure not to have any movement with your elbow joint. Some people rotate the dumb bell on the way down until your hands are aligned like you are doing a bench press at the bottom of the arc, then slowly rotate back to the starting position at the top. Again, maintain the arc and don't bend your elbows. Hug the tree. This exercise concentrates on your chest. Again, do a 10-8-6 and move up on dumb bell weight 5 lbs. for each set.

Overhead fly (optional): When I was very serious about working out, I really wanted to nail my chest and did these to work my lower chest. They work and get you ripped. This is optional, and if you are time constrained, don't worry about it.

Use one dumbell and set it on the floor "on end" at the head of a bench. Lie down on the bench and reach over your head and down to the dumbell and cup the one end of it. You then lift the dumbell in an arch (no elbow movement) until the dumbell is over your face. Do a 10-8-6 adding 5 pounds each time. This exercise concentrates on your lower chest.

Military Press: This is done sitting on a special rack with a bar and plates behind you at neck level. Normally you use a 45 pound bar, but I've seen special 35 lb. straight bars on these racks. Same deal, 10-8-6, adding 5 lbs. for each set. This exercise builds your front shoulder and tricep.

Shoulder Flys (optional): This exercise is done standing with dumbells. Maintain good posture. The rep starts with the dumbells at your belt buckle and you maintain a "hug the tree" arc in your arms. Extend the dumbells out to almost shoulder level, maintaining the arc. No elbow flexing. 10-8-6., increasing 5 lbs. a set. This exercise works on the middle of your shoulder.

Ropes: You use a pulley machine. The devise is a rope folded in two with each section roughly 18 inches in length with a clip for the cable in the center. The ropes start about chest high. Grab each rope and start with your arms at a 90 degree bend extending out in front of you. Pull the ropes down and spread them as you go down. Keep your elbows at the same level. This exercise really hits your triceps.

Abs: I found that 3 sets of 20 crunches gives me plenty of definition. If you want to really get cut, add reverse crunches. Lie down on an incline bench with your head on the high side, feet together below you. Barely lift your feet off the bench, and bring your legs up so your knees almost touch your gut. Return to the starting position, but don't rest your feet on the bench. Keep them off the bench.

(Tuesday, Friday)

Upright rows: After bench, my favorite exercise and highly underrated. Use a 25 lb. curl bar and plates. This exercise is done standing. Bend down and get a comfortable grip on the inside curls of the bar. Start out standing straight with the bar at belt buckle level. Raise the bar until it is slightly over your chin, then lower it. This exercise hits your center shoulder (delts), biceps, forearms, and traps (sides of your neck). An important tip, allow the bar to roll in your hands.

Curls: Done standing. Use the curl bar. Start with the bar basically touching your thighs, palms out. Keeping your elbows at the same level, raise (curl) the bar until it is almost touching your shoulders. The critical point is to keep your elbows in the same spot, otherwise you will cheat with your shoulder muscles. Also, don't swing with your knees to cheat it. Curls build the bicep and forearms.

One variant is the preacher curl, where you stand with your elbows on a special pad (pulpit). This requires your buddy to hand you the bar to begin. Another variant we invented that builds massive biceps is to start with the preacher pad in front of a pulley machine. You use massive weight and start with only a small angle, that is your hands upright and extended perhaps a foot out from your shoulders. Your buddy has to struggle to get the bar to you, then you crank the bar up to your shoulders. This requires very little movement and requires massive weight, but really cuts your biceps. Another variant uses dumbells. The main muscle worked is the bicep.

Rows: The variant I use is to go to a bench with a dumbell on the floor. For the right arm, put your left knee and foot on the bench, and your left hand, palm down. Reach down and pick up the dumbell. The exercise is like starting a lawn mower, pulling the dumbell up to your chest. Maintain a flat back, parallel with the bench during the rep. This exercise concentrates on the back part of your shoulder (delts) and also works your bicep. Another variant uses a pulley machine whereby you sit down and "start the lawn mower" using cables.

Lat machine: It is a machine, but this is done sitting with your knees under some pads. You reach up with a wide grip (past your shoulders) and pull the bar down to the back of your neck. This gives you better control than traditional pull ups, and when you get strong, pull ups are too easy and you need the machine to stack the weight. Note you can get a great lat work out just doing pull ups, so stick with them if you prefer.

Shrugs: This rack uses a 45 lb. bar with plates resting on two rails that you stand between. Grab the bar, palms facing back and shrug keeping your arms straight and locked. The shrug is a rolling motion lifting the bar. This exercise has little movement, but it targets your traps.

Calves: You use the shrug rack, and stand with the bar. You then stand on your tip toes then lower back down. This exercise targets your calves.

Legs (work in twice per week)

I admit I don't work a lot on my legs. I have a congenital knee deformation whereby my leg muscles connect to the inside of my knees and I have what is called a "tracking problem". This results in inflammation and pain when I do leg work outs, so I keep it light.

Leg Extension: This is done on a bench with special foot pads connected to a weight stack via pulleys. You sit down on the end of the bench and tuck your feet under the pads. You then extend your legs until they are straight out. This works the front of your upper legs.

Leg Curl: This is done on the same bench as the leg extensions. You lie flat on the bench on your stomach and hook your ankles behind the pads. You then curl with your legs until your feet almost touch your butt. This works out the back of your thighs and your butt.

Other:

Dead Lifts: I currently do dead lifts for my leg work out. As a warning, please note that a lot of people hurt themselves doing them. If you want to try them, make sure you get good training on technique and maintain proper posture. Basically you load up a bar and put it on the ground. With perfect posture you bend your knees and pick up the bar. Then you stand straight up with the bar. This works out the back of your legs and butt. I also do two shrugs with every lift to get a combo exercise in (builds your traps).

Squats: I don't do squats because of my knees. If you want to do them, again get good training and maintain proper posture. This is another exercise where people injure themselves. This works your legs and butt.

<u>Good Nutrition:</u> Eating right is critical for developing the physical side of frame. If you don't eat correctly you will have low energy, poor health, and you will be pudgy, which women don't like. Fortunately discoveries over the past decade have shown that eating what men naturally love to eat, e.g. meat and fat, is good for you.

Your diet should be a high fat, moderate protein diet, along with vegetables and some fruit. If you want more particulars, check out the Atkins diet or the Caveman diet. The key is to avoid carbohydrates, especially sugars. For fats, you want animal fat, butter, avocados, and coconut oil. You can have a little vegetable oil, though olive oil is better. For cooking stick to butter or coconut oil.

The bulk of your food should be animal meat. Beef, pork, chicken, fish, eggs, sausages, ham, bacon, steaks, ribs; it's all good so eat up. You should also eat nuts, which are high fat, moderate protein, as well as drink some milk and eat some cheese. Finally eat your vegetables like broccoli, beans, peas, carrots, and spinach. Salads are excellent, and remember to add some olive oil on top.

It is important to understand why this works. What you are battling is insulin and what you are raising is leptin. God gave us insulin for the fall harvest, and insulin gets mass produced when glucose is high in your bloodstream. When high carbohydrate, high sugar products are widely available, insulin converts these carbs into stored body fat while also suppressing the feeling of "fullness" allowing you to store away fat for the winter. Leptin gives you the fullness feeling and is suppressed by insulin. Leptin is boosted by eating fat and some protein. If you want to investigate this, next time you are hungry eat a small handful of almonds and then see what happens to your appetite 10 minutes later. Peanuts and sunflower seeds also work.

If you are young and work a physical job, you can have some carbs. Preferably go with whole grains such as whole grain bread. I am not as strict with carbs as others and it works for me, but there is nothing wrong with going full blown Atkins if you can stick to it. The acid test is to weigh yourself. If you are in shape, then your diet is working for you.

There are certain things you absolutely have to avoid due to the health problems: high fructose corn syrup (most drinks), sugar (candy), and trans-fats (hydrogenated fats). Eating too many carbs like bread, pasta, and potatoes is also something to avoid as they quickly convert to sugar and spike your insulin. This eventually leads to Type II diabetes and a host of other problems like clogged arteries, weight gain, low energy, stroke, high blood pressure, and other diseases. The big offender is sugary drinks. There are many diet drinks like Coke Zero that taste really good, so this is a big improvement you can make today with little effort just by switching. I don't trust the sweeteners they use, so the goal is to only drink milk and water, but I'll take Splenda over high fructose corn syrup any day.

Next is your vitamin stack. At a minimum you should take one multi vitamin/multi mineral a day. Even a Flinstones Chewable Complete is better than nothing. The problem is not eating enough vegetables, and also trace mineral depletion in our soils. Below is my vitamin stack. Feel free to investigate further and fine tune it, but it will work for you as-is to keep you healthy.

- Men's multi-vitamin / multi-mineral. Bulk of your B vitamins along with trace minerals. Make sure it does not contain iron, which is bad for men. You'll get all the iron you need from meat.
- Magnesium Glycinate, a.k.a. chelated magnesium. This is probably one of our biggest deficiencies. Note that Magnesium Oxide is poorly absorbed.
- Calcium/Magnesium/Zinc pill. The magnesium in this formulation is only partially absorbed, but it is a good source for calcium and zinc.
- Beta Carotene liqui-gel.
- Vitamin D-3, 2,000 i.u. liqui-gel.
- Flax Oil liqui-gel. Good source of A.L.A., a required fatty acid. Also known as an omega 3 fat.
- Vitamin B-12. This vitamin can be hard to absorb in some people. The chewable form absorbs well through your mouth.
- Vitamin C
- Vitamin K2 liqui-gel, or mixed K liqui-gel.

<u>Percent Body Fat:</u> This is an easy one. This means finding out your percent body fat and keeping it under control. What gets tracked gets controlled. I target 12-15% for myself. Younger men looking to attract females should stick to the lower side, though I think 10% is as low as you want to go. Older married men look good a little higher. My personal goal is 14%. There

is an easy way to do this, and that is with a pictogram. Simply use images.google.com and search "Percent Body Fat". There are many charts available, so pick the one you like and download it. Once a week stand in front of the mirror and check out the cues in the pictogram to make your judgment. This is a "good enough" method that works.

Aerobic Capacity: I define Aerobic Capacity as the ability to maintain a moderate level of physical exertion for an extended period, say 1 hour. For example you should be able to help you buddy install a new roof while only taking a break every hour. As a man you need to have this ability in reserve for you never know when you will be called upon for manly activity. Note Aerobic Capacity is also a key element if you ever get into a fight.

In order to build Aerobic Capacity it is important to bring your heart rate up then maintain it there. At a bare minimum you should target walking at a brisk pace for 2 miles, and do this 3 times a week. This is the bare minimum, but will probably put you in the top 20% of 20 yr. old men with regards to Aerobic Capacity. Add to this a little cheat: whenever you drive anywhere that has a parking lot, park in a space far away from where you are going, i.e. at the back of the lot. It helps.

An easy way to build Aerobic Capacity is with High Intensity wind sprints. This also boosts testosterone. The exercise involves sprinting full-out for 30 seconds, walking briskly for 90 seconds, then repeat. Do this so that you sprint (4) times. Add it up and its only 8 minutes. Again, doing this will put you in the top 20% among men.

Preferably you should do things like swimming (which can be inconvenient to do), biking, and hiking. In order to set your pace check your pulse and target around 120 beats per minute. Maintain that for a good 30 minutes and you'll be getting a good work out. Again 3 times per week is sufficient, but you can do more if you like. Note I recommend against jogging as it is not good for your knees. Brisk walking is much preferred and use a treadmill if you want.

Hygiene: Hopefully most men reading this don't require any help in this department, but there's probably a few that need to tune this up. In a nutshell, Don't Smell. Take a shower every day and make sure to wash your armpits and groin well. If you have acne, use a system like ProActiv and keep your face from looking oily. Also, make sure to use a deodorant. I prefer classic scent Old Spice.

Personal Appearance: It is important to present a good image of yourself to the outside world, and especially the ladies (even your wife). As a side benefit looking good helps strengthen the emotional side of frame. I've subdivided this section into sub sections:

1. Hair cut: The king of the men's hair cut is Brad Pitt. There are three good styles he has worn in movies that you can choose from if you are just getting started. First there is the spike, which you can find by image searching "Brad Pitt Fight Club". This should only be worn by younger men. The second is a hard core hair cut you can find by image searching "Brad Pitt Fury". The third is a more traditional hair cut you can find by image searching "Brad Pitt Inglorious".

2. Facial hair: If you are after the ladies, or want to keep your wife excited, go with the 5 o'clock shadow look. You'll have to buy special trimmers to maintain it. It is important to use them every morning or your look will degrade. You can try a mustache or short beard also. Be brutally honest with yourself when evaluating the look of a beard.

3. Color Scheme: I was schooled in this by my late wife. There are certain colors that go with your skin color. As a cheat sheet if you have olive or tan skin, you can wear white and black shirts. If you have pinker skin, then you have to go with pastels and grays. As an example someone who has pink skin should not wear a white dress shirt. Instead you might wear a light olive shirt or gray. In order to nail this down go to the men's department at a fine store and ask one of the dudes what shirt colors you should wear, and more importantly what colors you should avoid. The technical term is your "color palette". This little trick will help you get an edge in picking out good looking clothing.

Another option is to ask a girl at a make-up counter in a high-end store to determine your color palette. She will definitely know. Tell her you are mainly interested in shirts. Do this during an off hour as people might think you are a fag. You only have to do this once, so get it over with.

4. Clothes: This is a critical area that you need to work at. Unfortunately my look is "oil field worker grunge chic" and I usually wear boots and jeans. My shirts all have a "Carhardt" tag on them. This can work and I've gotten attention from ladies for this look, but I'm in the position of a widower who is a confirmed bachelor going forward, and frankly I go for comfort only. If you are a young man looking to slay the ladies, you have to reach higher.

On this note a lot of the sporting wear clothing / work style clothing actually looks really good, especially if you have a V shaped upper body that is ripped.   So don't overlook places like Cabella's and Bass Pro Shops to find some good looking clothes at a reasonable price. A masculine shirt you need to know about is called the "Henley". The key is to choose quality cloth when buying one. And this brings up a good point: make sure you buy quality clothing made from quality cloth.

The easiest way to improve your wardrobe is to observe other men who wear a masculine look and have "leveled up". Get some ideas then try to duplicate the look. Make sure to pay attention to shoes. I recommend going with a classy look rather than trendy. For example when the hipster look was popular, you would have done well to have avoided it. Imagine going on your motorcycle to a party full of hipsters in skinny jeans, and you show up with a Brad Pitt haircut, traditional quality clothing, and bulging biceps. You sir would have attracted all of the ladies.

One final thing, get yourself a nice suit with appropriate dress shirt that goes with your skin color. Get into the habit of wearing this to church and nicer affairs such as a fine dining date. Spend time researching what is classy and looks good. Don't be afraid to try on different suits until you can settle for the best one. This will be your most expensive purchase, so take a little time picking one out.

<u>Martial Arts:</u> Once you have developed your muscles, raised your energy levels with good nutrition, and have increased your Aerobic Capacity, it will be important for you to learn how to use these elements to defend yourself if the need should arise. Learning a fighting style will also strengthen the emotional side of your frame by boosting confidence. Below I discuss the various styles. Choose at least one and develop your fighting ability.

Grappling. Grappling is good for fighting in limited circumstances. In a "fair" fight (e.g. the tap-out rule is respected) where you know you won't get jumped by others, a grappler will generally win against an <u>untrained</u> opponent. Second, in all cases grappling teaches you an instinctive reflexive action if you are grabbed or someone attempts to tackle you. Third, in some grappling styles you are taught submission holds and locks which can be useful. In a "fair" fight certain submission holds end the fight. In a real fight, you would go all the way and dislocate joints or fracture bones. I want to recount two "fights" I got in where I used my wrestling skills.

The first fight was a classic one-on-one fight where no one was going to jump in. My opponent was a good 4 inches taller and had at least 40 lbs. on me. We started with a fist fight, and he quickly realized I knew what I was doing. Correctly gauging his size advantage, he attempted to tackle me. I countered and even landed a few jabs to his face, so he gave that up. I even remember telling him, "I'm a wrestler you dumb ass.". So we went back to a fist fight. He landed a good one to my face, but I made him pay for it. We both agreed to end the fight with no clear winner and actually had good relations afterward.

In the second instance my buddy decided it was time for some horseplay, so he attempted to tackle me in a work trailer. This was a good 15 years after I had last trained. I don't know what I did, but he went flying and slammed into the wall. That ended that. Thankfully there wasn't a desk between him and the wall or he would have been hurt. As it was, he didn't suffer any serious damage.

I hope these examples give you an idea of how grappling gives you an advantage. Let's review the styles:

1. Judo. Classic grappling. Great for a "fair" fight. The throws (while standing) work for all fights. Underrated style and I consider it the best all-around grappling style which is effective in fair fights and real fights. To the extent it teaches throws better than BJJ, it is superior in a real fight. In a real fight the ground game is worthless. In that situation you would

use a judo move to throw your opponent into a wall, table, or floor. This keeps you on your feet.

2. Brazilian Jui Jitsu. Highly overrated due to the success of it in MMA. For a "fair" fight, it is very good, perhaps even the best style unless going up against a trained striker. However it teaches you to go to the ground, and it makes you follow rules. This will get you destroyed in a bar brawl. Going to the ground? Insane. The locks and submission holds do have some application if you can get them while standing. All in all Jui Jitsu is a good style and worth learning.

3. American Wrestling. See the above stories for real world experience. Good for escaping getting grabbed, and works well in a "fair" fight. In a brawl, not particularly useful. A nice thing about wrestling is that it is oftentimes free by joining clubs at your university or a local club. See if you can get into some wrestling.

4. Aikido. Aikido gets a bad wrap for MMA ring matches and deservedly so, however Aikido can provide some benefit because it KEEPS YOU OFF THE GROUND. However this is not a particularly good self defense style.

Works in a "fair" fight, but also in a brawl if you get jumped and there are others around. Practice the simple moves and get good at them. The complex stuff is worthless. It also teaches submission locks; however in a brawl, you have to take it all the way and dislocate a joint if you are in danger of getting jumped, as in, you might die. Should be combined with training in striking to be truly effective. In a "real" fight, if you come up against someone experienced at striking, you'll probably get destroyed.

Striking. Much more relevant than grappling to real world situations. I'd emphasize hand attacks over kicking.

1. Boxing: The classic. Boxing is very good for street fighting as it teaches you to hit hard, use continuous combinations (lacking in a lot of martial arts), block, and to have good foot work. It also features a lot of sparring which is critical.

2. Wing Chun: This is the martial art popularized by Bruce Lee. It stresses hand attacks and blocking. It has application in street fights, especially if sparring is utilized heavily. Certain dojos concentrate on training hard on the applicable moves, which would be a great find.

3. Kemp Po or Kenpo: This is the Japanese style. When you think about "karate", this is what you are imagining. It's a decent style, especially if there is a lot of sparring (as opposed to "point matches"). It will certainly give you an advantage in a fight.

4. Tung Soo Do: Korean Kung Fu. Not a bad style that combines hand attacks, kicks, submission locks, and blocking as well as heavy sparring. I trained in this style and found it applicable to street fights. I know of one member in my club that used it in a fight and destroyed his opponent. Again make sure you get a lot of sparring, otherwise it is not very good.

5. Tae Kwon Do: This is the least desirable. It is Korean Karate that emphasizes kicking. A mean spinning back kick is the least useful in a typical bar fight, though a hard front kick is a good way to start a fight. Unfortunately this is what is most popular and all that may be available. If this is your only choice go ahead and sign up for it. Make sure to spar a lot.

6. Muay Thai / Kickboxing: This is an excellent style, but oftentimes hard to find. A lot of MMA fighters started with American Wrestling or Jui Jitsu, and then learned Muay Thai.

7. Kali: If you are interested in pure self defense, Kali is the best. This is a brutal style that emphasizes weapons, especially knives. It teaches you to conceal knives and deploy them quickly, then immediately go to carving up your opponent. This has very limited use in a "fair fight" (they do teach strikes), but it is brutal for real fights because that is what it is designed for. Note you will probably end up in lock-up after using it, so make darn sure you have a solid self-defense case if you use it. I consider this life-or-death type fighting – you were warned.

Side Two: Spiritual

If you are a practicing Catholic, chances are you already have a decent Spiritual Side of frame, certainly stronger than other men. However being a decent Catholic is not enough to live a fulfilling life, so I present to you the following to develop a solid Spiritual side of frame.

The Basics:

1. Stop sinning. This is where it begins. If you are committing mortal sins you will not progress as you are cut off from Grace. In order to overcome sin, you will need weekly confession and prayer. Have hope, the Lord will give you the Grace to succeed, so keep at it until you avoid mortal sin. Afterward confession every 2-3 weeks seems optimal.

2. Prayer: Pray on your knees in the morning (at a minimum, say the morning offering), and before bed (at a minimum an act of contrition). I also recommend some free flowing prayer where you thank God for at least one blessing that happened during the day, and also ask for His help in one area. You should also consider a daily 5-decade rosary (without all of the Novus Ordo adders). If you can't do a daily rosary, then at least say one during the weekend. Note: Prayer should not be a torture session. If you are spending hours in prayer chances are you suffer from what is called scruples. Talk to your priest about this and adjust your prayer life so that it conforms to your State in Life. This means that you should not have the prayer life of a monk if you are a single man who wants to get married and provide for a large Catholic family.

A quick test to determine if you have scruples is to limit your prayers to (1) morning offering and (1) act of contrition a day for one week. If you start dreading that you are sinning and going to hell for doing this, you have scruples.

Another element of prayer life is the prayer before meals. Yes, this means if you are out with your buddies at a restaurant, you WILL cross yourself and thank the Lord for your food. You will also do this at business functions, the college cafeteria, etc.... Don't be a damned sissy.

3. The Sacraments: Communion at least once per week, and Confession every two weeks to monthly. If you are combating a particular sin, then weekly Confession is a great tool. I highly advise that you track down a Traditional chapel run by the SSPX, FSSP, or ICKSP (Institute of Christ the King). "Diocesan" Trad Masses are usually good, but they can be a mixed bag. The Novus Ordo in most cases is deleterious to your Faith.

4. Fasting: Fasting is a great way to develop spiritually. I personally like a once-per-week electronics fast. As a Catholic you should also abstain from meat on Fridays. Another easy fast is to skip breakfast once per week, and to delay lunch until an hour later than normal. There is no need to over complicate fasting. Also note that breaking a fast is not mortal sin, so do not let the fear of sinning prevent you from attempting to fast.

<u>Spiritual Reading:</u>

Below are some suggestions to get you started.

1. Thomas Aquinas. His writings are available online. Feel free to read sections out of order that appeal to you. Titles to check out include *Summa Theologica*, *Summa Contra Gentiles*, and *De Veritate* (*Questiones Disputatae de Veritate*)

2. Josef Pieper. *On Hope* and *The Four Cardinal Virtues*. I consider *The Four Cardinal Virtues* mandatory reading.

3. Edward Feser. Great works of his: *The Last Superstition*, *Scholastic Metaphysics*, *Aquinas*, and *Philosophy of the Mind*. As of this writing he also maintains a blog. Search "Edward Feser Blog" and you will find it. If you come into frequent contact with atheists, *The Last Superstition* is mandatory reading.

4. Fr. Chad Ripperger. Fr. Ripperger has given many talks which are available as audio files and via YouTube. I highly recommend "How to Raise a Man."

5. Fr. Isaac Relyea. Fr. Issac has given many talks that are available on the internet. He is known for his "fire and brimstone" approach.

6. The Bible. For online reading use drbo.org. For a print version use the Douay Rheims edition.

7. Robert Sungenis. *Not By Faith Alone* is in a league of its own when it comes to Catholic apologetics.

8. *Where We Got the Bible* by Graham, available from TAN books. An excellent book on history and apologetics with regards to the bible.

These are enough to get you started. After you get into the habit of including some spiritual reading in your life, add other works. Reading about various Saints is also very profitable.

<u>Virtues:</u>

The penultimate goal for Catholics is to develop a life of virtue. Developing virtues requires (3) important steps:

1. Prayer. Pray to God to give you grace to develop a particular virtue.

2. Fasting. During your weekly fast offer it up to receive grace for a particular virtue.

3. Practice. We talk about "the habit of virtue". To develop a good habit it is important to repeat an act until it becomes more or less automatic. Therefore find ways to do the virtuous actions corresponding to the virtue you are trying to develop.

Learn about the various virtues and pick a few to work on. *The Four Cardinal Virtues* by Pieper lists many virtues and vices, so I consider this mandatory reading. While researching a virtue, pay attention to the corresponding vices of deficit and excess, as this will shed more light on what is involved with a particular virtue.

Here is a list of virtues with a short description that you should consider:

1. Charity. The eternally enduring Theological Virtue and the most important to have. At its core this is the Love of God. To develop this virtue, practice doing things with the Love of God in mind. If you help out a stranger, say a silent prayer: "For Jesus". You should also contemplate on how much God loves you. Contemplating the Cross is a good practice in this regard.

2. Prudence. One of the four Cardinal Virtues, it has the pride of place. Prudence means aligning yourself with reality. An example of Prudence would be accepting that you took a worthless degree in college and won't be able to support a family. You would then investigate ways to acquire training such that you can obtain work that pays you enough so that you can get married. As an aside, if this is a problem you have, consider reading the book *Worthless* by Aaron Clarey.

3. Magnanimity. Believing in great things and doing great things. Many Catholics of the neo-Jansenist bent are shocked that this is a Catholic Virtue. Magnanimity at its core realizes that Life is wonderful and beautiful. People who are magnanimous celebrate Life and enjoy producing value. An example of a magnanimous act is reading this book so that you can have a productive life. The vice of deficit is worth mentioning – pusillanimity. This is the vice of hand-wringing and excuse making. Every Catholic man should work hard to develop the virtue of Magnanimity.

4. Humility. A Catholic man can only progress if he is humble. Only a humble man can be magnanimous, and only a humble man can learn from his mistakes. Humility at its core is admitting to yourself that you have faults. There is a grave error in thinking that humility means believing you are worthless. Unfortunately many men will reject humility due to this misunderstanding, because what they are rejecting is the vice of false humility.

From God's perspective humility is the realization that God owes us nothing. We can not add to God's existence, nor can we take away from it. Compared to God we are nothing. From man's perspective humility means knowing your proper place and owning your mistakes. There's an old saying about a mistake, "learn or lose". When you own your mistake, you can learn from it and improve. Note you don't have to air your dirty laundry -- leave that to the confessional. However always admit to yourself when you have screwed up. With regards to others, admit when you are wrong, don't be an excuse maker, and don't lie. I can not stress this enough, humility is the key that opens the door to a masculine life.

5. Diligence. This is an important virtue if you want to be successful. Diligence means getting things done immediately. One thing that can dissuade a man is a complex project

spanning weeks with multiple steps. The important part to dealing with a complex project is to develop a plan with actionable items, then always moving the next step to your daily schedule/list.

A great help for developing Diligence is a book entitled *Getting Things Done* by David Allen. One of the greatest tools I took away from the book was the "Waiting On" list. Many times you have something on your to-do list, e.g. "call the bank". You execute, but are told they will have to get back to you. Very quickly your to-do list will get cluttered with items you need to accomplish, however they are not currently actionable. In cases like these you move the item to "Waiting On", then review that list every few days to see if follow up calls are needed. I've used this system for multi-million dollar projects and was amazed at how well it worked. I highly recommend this book as it will assist you greatly in developing Diligence.

6. Fortitude. This is the virtue to bravely tackle adversity. A good way to develop Fortitude is to try and fail. When you realize that your can handle failure, your Fortitude will strengthen. Josef Pieper goes in depth on Fortitude, so be sure to read his book "The Four Cardinal Virtues".

7. Temperance. Temperance is self control in consuming things. This includes alcohol, snacks, drugs, and entertainment. In order to develop this virtue you must develop a life of fasting. Again Josef Pieper discusses this virtue in depth.

Side Three: Intellectual

The human mind is composed of the will, emotions, and the intellect. The will is strengthened by the Virtues, and for emotions, which is a side of Frame, I have devoted a section in this book. That leaves intellect.

It is important for us to have knowledge and wisdom so that we may live by right reason. This means we must have a strong intellect. For wisdom this comes through experience, and also philosophy. For knowledge, we must continually learn about the world around us. Note that this is a life-long endeavor, so pace yourself.

When it comes to philosophy, there is only one school that is internally consistent and provides a complete model for existence, and that is Greek Realism, and in particular Aristotelian / Thomistic philosophy. It is incumbent upon the Catholic man to at least become familiar with this philosophy.

There is overlap between the Spiritual Side of Frame and the Intellectual Side when it comes to philosophy. The reading list I provided under the Spiritual Side is the same. To begin, read *The Last Superstition* by Feser and then his *Aquinas*. After reading these books, move on to studying the works of Aquinas himself. Finally go back to Feser and read *Philosophy of the Mind*.

When it comes to knowledge, in the age of Amazon, Kindle, YouTube, and the internet in general, there is no limit. I'll make some suggestions to help get you started.

I think the easiest way to start fostering intellectual pursuits is through history. A good place to begin is with war documentaries, available on YouTube and Netflix. Spend an hour or two during your leisure Sunday time to watch a documentary or two.

When it comes to history I highly recommend the author Carroll and his *The Last Crusade*, which is about the Spanish Civil War, *The Guillotine and the Cross*, about the French Revolution, and finally his *The Rise and Fall of the Communist Revolution*.

On economics I recommend my book *The Economics of Catholic Subsidiarity* which tackles economics from a Catholic perspective. Available on Amazon.

Every Catholic should be familiar with our mortal enemy, communism, so I recommend *Radical Son* and *Politics of Bad Faith* by David Horowitz. I also recommend watching documentaries on The Frankfurt School and Cultural Marxism on YouTube. Finally, be sure to watch the interview and lectures given by Yuri Bezmenov, again available on YouTube.

You will also want to learn new skills. On the internet Udemy is a paid service with countless subjects. Prices are cheap. A free service that is excellent is Khan's academy. It covers a vast multitude of topics, mostly centered around mathematics. You should also learn mechanical skills, which skills are taught for free on YouTube.

For politics, I recommend Ayn Rand's *Atlas Shrugged* and *The Fountainhead*. Note she was a Greek Realist AND an atheist (talk about contradiction) and blames the world's problems on the belief in Original Sin. If you are a strong Catholic, you will laugh at the atheism part of her argument in *Atlas Shrugged* (known as John Galt's Speech) as she presents a dystopian world, a world of Fallen Man (the irony). Actually you can skip John Galt's Speech in *Atlas Shrugged* and you miss nothing. Anyhow, she shows how getting away from Greek Realism is the culprit for the world's woes, and this takes up 95% of *Atlas Shrugged*. *The Fountainhead* is less about politics and more about the nihilism and leftist hatred of beauty. Both are worth reading.

I think young men should also work on computer literacy. I have found the Sam's books to be well written, e.g. *Sam's Teaches You Python*. Udemy also offers courses ranging from web development to coding, to Word Press, to networking.

You may consider learning a foreign language like Spanish, French, or Latin. There are online sites that teach this.

This is just a small taste of what is out there. Again the goal is to make this a life long endeavor. Pace yourself and work on continuing to develop your knowledge base. Note also that developing a strong intellectual life will make you a more interesting person and is useful when it comes to having conversations with your peers and the ladies.

Side Four: Emotional

I have saved the best for last. Besides the Physical/Body Side of Frame the modern young man is oftentimes lacking in the Emotional Side. In fact the internet has coined a term for the physically and emotionally weak young man – the soyboy. This is derived from the claim that soy estrogens are lowering the testosterone in men. As you can imagine women detest soyboys.

A man who has developed the Emotional Side of his Frame is confident, at ease, and seems to exude positive energy. He is mature and not derailed when he makes a mistake or faces hardship. It is said of him that he has an abundance mindset and provides value to people. At the same time, he is the predator, not the prey when it comes to opposition. In short, he is a man.

The soyboy is the consummate needy whiner and excuse maker. He accomplishes very little because he rarely tries. Women lead him instead of him leading women, and a common trait in his interaction with the ladies is to blow up their phones with text messages (which is gay). He is the pusillanimous metrosexual that should be put out of its misery.

To begin, Emotional Frame depends on the other three sides of frame, especially Physical/Body and Spiritual. If you dress well, have a "V" shape, and are practiced in a fighting style, you will have confidence. If you are strong in the Spiritual Side of Frame, you will be progressing in the Virtues which allows you to keep your emotions in check. The Intellectual Side is not quite as important, but knowing how to handle yourself with interesting conversations will boost your confidence.

Besides the crossover from the other sides of Frame, there are deliberate steps you can take to strengthen the emotional side of

Frame which I will now present. Note that doing this program will take about a year, but along the way you will see positive results. Note you will have to purchase and read these books if you want to improve:

1. Motivation. Start off by reading *Rogue Warrior* by Rick Marcinko. This book will definitely get you pumped.

2. Intro. Read the book *Gorilla Mindset* by Mike Cernovich. This is a short book with some exercises in it. This will get you in touch with the importance of a healthy emotional life, especially in establishing a positive mindset and an abundance mentality.

3. Application. This is a program created by the Wolf of Wallstreet that motivates you to get things done:
   a. Purpose. Think about the purpose for what you are doing, e.g. you are going to college so that you can get a good job that allows you to support a large Catholic family.
   b. Vision. Spend some time thinking about what success looks like vs. what failing will look like. Go into some detail. For example, if I get good grades and land a high paying job, in a few years I'll be married to a hot little Trad girl who likes to wear an apron and heels as she cooks my dinner. If I fail, in a few years I'll be a pissed soaked drunk living in a rented single wide trailer. Spend some time each day visualizing what each looks like.
   c. State Control. This overlaps with the book *Gorilla Mindset*. Work on maintaining a positive mindset. Analyze your thoughts and stamp out negative self talk. Replace it with detailed positive thoughts: "I am a great student and I'm going to kill it today." Another practice is to smile a few times a day. Force it and see what happens – your mood improves.

    d. Plan. Make a detailed plan on how you will achieve your vision and complete your purpose. E.g., I will study from 4 to 5:30, then break until 7. I'll then study until 9. I will be in bed by 10:30 and get a good night's sleep.
    e. Hard Work. After you have the proper mindset, execute. Do it. Remember success feeds off of itself.
    f. Set realistic stretch goals. You know that for an engineer, a 3.2 GPA will get you a good job. Set a stretch goal to beat a 3.5 GPA.

4. Advanced Training. There is a book called *The Nine Laws* by Ivan Throne. Ivan lived a few years at a Ninja temple and became a black belt in Ninjitsu. The major focus of his training was emotional strength. The book is his attempt to convert the Ninja beliefs to the Western world. In the book he presents a program for developing emotional strength.

His discussion on the Ninja beliefs are interesting, but it is my opinion you can go right to the program. In my edition this starts at Chapter 24 on page 249 and goes until Chapter 29, roughly 70 pages. I would set a goal to work through one chapter per month. As an added bonus he has chosen the medieval art known as Danse Macabre to illustrate his book. I'll also note that there is nothing in the program objectionable to Catholics such as Eastern mysticism, etc… It is pretty straight forward.

Finally there is a forgotten concept known as esprit de corp. Esprit de corp is created by an all-male team in pursuit of an objective, and esprit de corp creates men. It is a virtuous cycle. On a team that has esprit de corp a rallying cry is often "I won't let you fail". Due to the importance of esprit de corp in developing as an emotionally strong man I highly recommend that young men should set a goal to work on an all male crew at least once in their lives, preferably in a manly profession; in fact I consider this mandatory. If you are in college, work one summer as an unskilled laborer in the oil fields, work on a ranch, work in logging, or work on a fishing boat. Get with a male crew and let them wipe the greenhorn out of you.

I'll give you some advice when it comes to hazing. All male crews with high esprit de corp will haze greenhorns. It is said on drilling rigs that the rig boss never fires anyone – his crew will run off the scrubs instead. Hazing is not a big deal and basically is used to teach you humility. The key is to do what you are told AND NEVER WHINE. After a few days the men will see you are not a pussy and they'll bring you into the team. As an added benefit all pride will be wiped away from you and you won't hesitate to ask questions. That is how you will learn.

In close, when developing Emotional Strength it is important to know what this looks like. It is a serious man that has a positive mindset, a can-do attitude who provides value to others. His source is Charity, the Love of God. He is rarely stressed, but not a slackard. He is confident. People are happy to be in his company and he oftentimes finds himself made the leader. This is your goal.

Section 2: Application

Once you have worked on your frame, you will want to apply it to living a rewarding life. In this section we'll address hobbies, skills and activities, education, and work life. Missing from this list is getting a woman. This will be discussed in a stand-alone section, but note having an interesting and productive life is key to attracting the females.

Hobbies:
In order to enjoy life, you have to LIVE life. Part of that is developing some interesting hobbies. The list is endless, however I've listed some below for you to consider. You should develop 2-3 hobbies at least.

1. Fishing. Fishing can be broken down to 3 types: trout fishing using a fly rod, salt water, and fresh water fishing going after bass and bream. Freshwater fishing is the easiest to get into, so that is what I will present.

The best way to get into freshwater fishing is to get help from a buddy. Barring that, here is a quick start guide.
Equipment:
      a. Shimano spinning reel. I prefer one with a trigger. You can use other brands if you want.
      b. Graphite rod, 5' - 10" with cork handle.
      c. 12 lb. test monofilament (nylon) line. 100 yards.
      d. A few packs of watermelon seed color "super flukes", available online from Walmart.
      e. A few packs of Berkely Power Worms, pumpkin seed color.
      f. 2/0 offset hooks, for flukes.
      g. 2/0 Tru-Turn worm hooks for worms.
      i. Pack of 1/8" ounce bullet weights.
      j. Tackle box.

Skills:

a. Learn to tie a hook. I prefer the twice through the eye cinch knot, but there are others such as the palomar knot. Consult online articles or Youtube.
b. Go on YouTube and search "carolina rig worm". Learn to rig up a carolina rig and fish with a worm.
c. Go on YouTube and seach for "Super Fluke" or "Jerk Bait". Learn how to rig a Super Fluke and fish with it.
d. Practice casting. Use a pond or a swimming pool. Tie a loop around (2) bullet weights and practice casting. Use YouTube if you need help casting a spinning reel.

Execute:

Get a fishing license from Walmart and find some lakes and ponds to go bass fishing. Use your skills and catch some bass. If possible go with a buddy on his boat. Also, feel free to fillet and eat some of your bass, they are good to eat.

After you increase in skill, consider going after bream, which are usually blue gills, or shell crackers/red ears. You use "ultralight" tackle to catch them. These fish are excellent to eat, but the trick is to catch ones big enough to fillet.

Another option is crappy fishing. This usually requires a boat, but crappy are probably one of the best eating fish you can catch.

Fishing is something you can do at anytime, and you can go solo and fish from shore. You can also buy a small pontoon boat equipped with an electric trolling motor to fish ponds. However the most fun is going fishing with your buddies.

2. Hunting This is a sport you definitely want to do with a buddy who can teach you. You can do some preliminary work beforehand, however, like acquiring a gun and learning marksmanship. I also highly recommend that you take a hunting/gun safety course from the NRA.

There are 4 types of hunting I'll discuss:
     a. Upland game hunting (quail/pheasant)
     b. Deer hunting
     c. Small game hunting
     d. Duck/Goose hunting.

Upland game hunting: For this style of hunting you will need a shotgun. A 12 gauge Remington 870 pump shotgun works fine and is a good all-around gun. The preferred shotgun is a two shot over/under shotgun. A semi-automatic will also work. If you are going after pheasant you will need N°. 4 high brass shells. For quail, use 7-1/2 shot. Before you start hunting acquire a trap table and a few boxes of clay pigeons. Practice leading the clay pigeons and keeping your gun in a swing while you shoot. After you can dust the clay pigeons, get with a buddy and see if you can go hunting. Hunting with dogs is especially fun.

Deer hunting: Again, best learned from a buddy. For preliminaries purchase a bolt action rifle chambered in 30-06 or 270. Make sure to also buy a scope. Join a gun range. Go on Youtube and learn how to "bore-site" the scope, then fine tune the scope at the gun range. Practice on targets at 100 yards. Finally, watch some videos on Youtube on how to skin a deer. When you kill your deer, I highly recommend getting the butcher to make you deer/pork sausage. They are excellent, especially smoked.

Small game hunting: Purchase a 22 rimfire rifle. The old standby is the Ruger 10/22 semi-automatic. Practice shooting, then hunt for rabbits and squirrels. Make sure to eat what you kill. Watch Youtube to learn how to skin them.

Duck/Goose hunting: You will definitely need a buddy who has a duck blind, dogs, and decoys. You will need a shotgun, preferably a semi-automatic, though a pump shotgun will work. Again, practice with clay pigeons before your first hunt. Duck hunting is usually done in cold, wet weather so make sure you get the proper clothing to stay warm.

3. Mountain Biking: I don't have any experience with this sport. All you need is the proper bike, a bike rack for your car, and some trails. I recommend checking out Youtube on buying the proper bike. As always, see if you can do this hobby with a buddy.

4. Motorcycle Riding: This is an excellent sport for men, and as an added bonus a motorcycle is catnip to the ladies.
   Equipment:
        a. Full helmet with visor. Getting hit in the face by a bug at high speeds really sucks.
        b. Leather jacket. Motorcycle jackets equipped with internal foam "armor" are the best. If you spend the money on a motorcycle jacket, make sure it has zippered vents. A regular leather jacket is good enough.
        c. Boots. Hiking boots work fine, but if you want to go hard core, get "engineer boots".
        d. Gloves. Get motorcycle gloves with "armor" on the knuckles.

   Training:
        a. While not necessary, I highly recommend learning how to drive a stick shift (manual transmission) car or truck. You should be able to start from a stopped position, and to shift into at least second gear. This

helps you understand the shifting concept and makes motorcycle training easier.
b. Motorcycle Safety Foundation training course, search for a local one with Google. The MSF course has the benefit that in most States if you pass the course, you automatically get a license. Note do not worry if you fail the course, as it is pretty intense. You will definitely know how to ride a motorcycle, and the local DMV riding test is so easy it is silly, even if you have failed the MSF course. If at all possible take this course.
c. Route driving, 45 mph max speed. Search your area and find a "square", preferably 1 mile to the side with good quality pavement. After you receive your license you should go out each day and "run the route". I'd do this for a good 100 miles before you progress to more difficult riding. Note that if you have a new bike, this is mandatory as this will allow you to limit your engine RPMs as you break-in your engine.
d. Circle drills. Find a large parking lot that is not busy. The goal is to ride in first gear near idle speed and do circles left and right with the handle bars locked full over to each side. You should drag your rear brake while doing this. Note this is done at very slow speed. After you can do circles, add in figure 8's, again locking the handle bars fully over until they hit the stops. This is an excellent exercise and I highly recommend doing it a few times per week until it becomes easy.
e. Curves. While you are practicing, keep a look out for a curvy road with good pavement and minimal traffic. After you have hit 100 – 200 miles "running the route", try out the curve run. At first take the curves on the slow side so it is easy. Practice counter steering and getting your hips into the turn. As you

gain confidence, increase the speed of your run to the speed limit.

Purchase:
    a. Decide on the style of bike that you want, either a sport bike or a cruiser. Sport's bikes are a lot of fun. Cruisers are great for longer distance rides, and they are better if you want to ride with your girlfriend/wife.
    b. For a sports bike, I recommend a 300 cc bike for a beginner. Two models I like are the Yamaha R3 and the Ninja 300. These bikes are very light and easy to learn on. They are also very popular so finding one used is relatively easy. Note if you buy a new bike, I recommend getting one with ABS for added safety.
    c. For a cruiser, I highly recommend the Kawasaki Vulcan S. This is a 650 cc bike that is a cross between a Cafe Racer and a Cruiser. It is a light bike that is easy to ride, perfect for a beginner. Also this is a popular bike, so picking up one used is not difficult. Note that the bike has incredible power, so take it easy while learning. Kawasaki has tuned the bike to top out at 110 mph, so the bike has a lot of power at lower speeds and accelerates like a beast. For this reason there is no reason to sell the bike once you become an intermediate rider. As a Cruiser it is relatively comfortable and has no problems maintaining highway speeds of 75 mph. If you have a wife or girlfriend make sure to get the passenger seat and foot pegs.

5. Camping

Camping is a fun hobby, especially when you go with your buddies. This is one of the easier hobbies to get into, so I recommend you give it a try if you are just starting out.

Equipment:
    a. Tent. I recommend a 3-man tent.
    b. Sleeping bag. Match the temperature rating for your location. Don't take an arctic bag out camping in the middle of the summer.
    c. Back pack.
    d. Butane stove. Butane cylinders are readily available at Walmart and sporting goods stores.
    e. Cooking gear.
    f. Cooler.

Locations:
    When just starting out, check out your State and County parks and look for a place that has an electrical outlet and water spigot at each campsite. This makes camping a breeze. It is also a lot of fun to combine fishing with camping, so check out local lakes that have campsites. Also check for any restrictions on alcohol usage. There is nothing like sitting around a campfire with your buddies and drinking a few beers.

Activites:
    a. Fishing.
    b. Swimming.
    c. Frisbee / other sports.
    d. Grilling. (Bring charcoal).
    e. Hiking.
    f. Lighting off a bonfire.
    g. Cooking hotdogs and marshmallows over the fire.

A lot of guys nowadays don't know how to start a fire, so I will go through it. First, understand the types of fuel: tinder, kindling, and wood. Tinder is very fine and easily lights. A good source of tinder is dryer lint, but you can use natural grasses that are brown and dry. Kindling are wood pieces the size of your thumb to a bit bigger. "Wood" or fuel is the main logs you will use on a fire and can burn up to an hour.

Start by making a pile of tinder, then build a kindling tee-pee around it, leaving an opening so you can light the tinder. I will usually build a 4-sided log cabin of wood around the tee-pee. Light off the tinder, and monitor the fire, adding additional tinder as needed. When you hear snapping and crackling, that is the kindling starting to burn. Slowly add kindling as needed. As the fire takes off, lay long pieces of kindling and some fuel logs across the log cabin. You now have a fire. Note a big mistake people make is to not leave gaps in the wood for air to enter. This is why you should try to maintain a log cabin stack around the fire with good sized gaps between the logs.

6. Horseback Riding.
    If you live in a rural area or near to one, consider horseback riding. It goes without saying that men ride Western, though we make an exception for our Brit buddies. If your buddy ranches or comes from a farming / ranching family, see if you can get him to teach you to ride a horse. When you become proficient you can go on trail rides through beautiful terrain, or sign up for a horse back guided hunt. As an added bonus taking a girl out on a horseback ride picnic will earn you a lot of points.

7. Mushroom Growing.
    I have actually tried this. Purchase an oyster mushroom kit from Amazon and give it a try. Oyster mushrooms are excellent when lightly fried and served with steak. If you like growing mushrooms, watch some Youtube videos and learn about growing without using a kit.

8. Beer Brewing

Similar to mushroom growing, purchase a kit from Amazon and try it out. If you have good results, consider watching some Youtube videos and work on brewing on your own.

9. Hiking

    This is an easy hobby to get into, and it is best done with your buddies. Purchase some light weight hiking boots, a small back pack, water bottle, and a decent camera. Check out your area for some scenic trails and spend the day hiking. This can also be combined with camping.

10. Sports

    Don't forget about sports. Look into golf, tennis, and softball, among others. I also like frisbee golf if a course is available near you.

This is a small list of hobbies you can explore. You can also look into fly tying, rock climbing (there are now a lot of indoor climbing centers available), gardening, woodworking, sky diving, astronomy, painting, etc.... Now consider, would your time be better spent pursuing some of these hobbies or playing video games? Also, after you have gotten into a few hobbies, imagine going out on a date and having an endless supply of interesting conversation topics with your girlfriend which will come from your hobbies. This is important lads.

Skills and Activities

1. Small repairs

    Every man should be able to handle small repairs around his house or apartment. To start, you will need to purchase a tool box and slowly stock it. To begin I would go with a hammer, Crescent wrench, Channel Lock pliers, 3/8" socket set, tape measure, and screwdrivers (regular and phillips). As you identify a needed repair, check out on Youtube on how to do it and acquire additional tools as needed.

    If you live in a house or rent one, I also recommend purchasing a tool chest and then augment your tool collection. Add in a 1/2" socket set as well as some box wrenches. I also have found a Stilsen wrench (pipe wrench) to be very useful. I recommend a few different sizes like the 14", and smaller. Also in this day and age a cordless drill/screw driver is a necessity. I like the DeWalt, Milwaulkee, Makita, and Hitachi brands. Bosch is a nice brand but seems overpriced.

    Here is a pro-tip if you own a lawn mower or riding mower. I have discovered the electric impact wrench. This device makes removing blades a piece of cake, and it also came in handy when I had to change a flat tire on a riding mower. I went with the 1/2" drive.

2. Car and Motorcycle repair

    Every man needs to learn how to maintain his car. At a minimum you should learn how to change your own oil/filter, change a tire, replace spark plugs, check/replenish other fluids, and replace a battery. For tire practice, jack up your car, remove a tire, and then reinstall it. Note oftentimes if you get a flat you can take the flat tire to the shop and get it plugged for $5, saving you a lot of money. You can also plug a tire yourself if you buy a kit.

If you own a motorcycle you will need additional tools such as a brass chain brush, chain wax, torque wrench, and hex head drivers. You should be able to clean your chain, lube your chain, tighten your chain, and change the oil. Consult your owners' guide and Youtube for help.

3. Grilling

I highly recommend that men learn how to grill out. You will have to decide on what type of grilling to do. A propane grill is the most convenient. A charcoal grill provides better flavor, but you have to remember to keep charcoal in stock, and you have to deal with ash disposal. For a limited budget and/or limited space, such as an apartment, a charcoal grill is probably the way to go. Note if you go the charcoal route, I recommend against the easy start briquets that have the lighting fluid impregnated into the briquet. This is because adding additional charcoal will introduce a nice lighter fluid taste to your meats.

To begin, start with hotdogs and hamburgers. Purchase frozen pre-made lean paddies from Walmart. The leaner the better, as this reduces the chance of the burgers catching on fire. Get your grill heated up, and then place still-frozen patties on the grill and close it. Cook for 7 minutes. Next, flip the patties and put on your hot dogs. You want your hotdogs to have some light charring, which has a great flavor. Cook for another 6 minutes, and you are done. If you want a cheeseburger, add a slice of provolone cheese 1 minute before you are done. Also lightly salt the burgers on each side.

After you have perfected grilling, have a cook out. Invite some buddies over and the ladies, and cook out some hamburgers and hotdogs. Everyone loves a cook out. Remember to instruct the ladies to provide side fixings like potato salad.

To progress, move to grilling steaks. Start with 7 minutes on one side and 6 minutes on the other to begin. I recommend sprinkling McCormick's Montreal Steak Spice on each side. Adjust your cooking times until you can cook the steak to the desired extent: well done, medium, rare, etc… Grilled steaks are excellent, though pricey. Go ahead and grill sirloin steaks and even pork chops to save money if needed.

4. Smoking

Smoking is a form of cooking meat popular in the South. The flavor is excellent when done correctly. You can purchase a large smoking rig, however the egg-style smaller units work well. The easiest meat to learn on is beef, such as a brisket or sirloin roast. Chicken is a little harder, and I have found that you need a higher temperature to make sure it cooks well. Ribs require roasting in the oven for a few hours, and then moving to the smoker. For wood I like pecan, mesquite, and hickory wood. For smoking it is best if you get help from a buddy, or spend some time on Youtube. Also experiment with different barbeque sauces and rubs. My preference is original Stub's.

5. Swing dancing

For young single men I consider swing dancing a necessary skill. There is nothing morally objectionable about it; even the music usually has no lyrics. Club / disco dancing sucks, is equivalent to simulated sex, and only fags can do a good job with it. Swing dancing is the way to go, and it is relatively easy to learn. Search for "East Coast Swing" and take some lessons. In the South if you like country music they have another version called "Texas Two Step" and "Southern Swing" that is also fun to learn.

6. Investing

As a man, you need to learn about investing. I recommend using a conservative approach as a beginner. To start, open an IRA account. A good firm with quality mutual funds is Vanguard. Contribute some money each year to this account. Invest half in a quality corporate bond fund, and half in stock funds. If you don't know what stock fund to use, then use the Vanguard S&P fund. Later start studying reports on funds and find ones you think are a good investment.

Another easy way to invest is to build a T-Bill Ladder. Open an account on TreasuryDirect.gov. You will need to know your bank account and routing number for your bank, both of which are listed on the bottom of your checks. Each month purchase a 6 month (26 week) T-Bill, which will cost $100. Enable "auto reinvest". After six months you have what is called a ladder, which means each month money will be available to you if you need it. If you don't need the money, you do nothing and it automatically reinvests in another 6 month T-Bill. If you need the money, say for a new tire, you cancel the reinvestment and take the money.

Keep adding $100 each month, and pretty soon you will have thousands of dollars saved up. This is a good way to save for the down payment on a house. Note you can invest more than $100, but this is the bare minimum.

Education

Unfortunately education is an area where many Catholic men make mistakes, oftentimes resulting in life long negative consequences. In most cases education should be used as a tool to get a job that allows you to comfortably support a large Catholic family with a stay-at-home mom. This means that a history degree or a philosophy degree won't work. Now there are some exceptions that I will discuss. If you can get a near 4.0 GPA at a highly ranked college and go on to get a PhD, you can end up with a tenured professorship and make some decent money. However 80 – 90% of men who get these degrees end up teaching at community colleges for $30K per year and struggle to support a family.

The only time I would recommend a man getting a liberal arts degree is if he will inherit the family business. In that case I think a philosophy degree coupled with an accounting minor would be a good fit. However I doubt many of my readers fit into this category. If you are considering college and have not started yet, I advise avoiding the liberal arts. Economics, Business Administration, and Finance are also degrees to avoid that many men make the mistake of taking.

Unfortunately many of my Catholic readers will be college aged men half way through a history degree or a philosophy degree. What do you do in that case? Use these guidelines:

1. Do you have a very high GPA (greater than 3.5)? If not, don't continue.
2. Is the college you are attending notable in this field or have some prestige? If not, don't continue.
3. Does a notable professor in the field know you by name? Has he invited you over for a party or some other gathering? Can you get in good with such a professor?

If you pass all of that, then you have a shot. Basically you are going to need a PhD and teach at a University that pays well. If this is the way you'll go, follow these guidelines:

1. Talk to your professor about your chances of getting a PhD. As a first step you will need a Master's, so talk about that also. You may come away realizing that this is not the path for you.

2. Network like there is no tomorrow. Attend conferences and talks at other universities and make connections. Leverage your prestigious professor to get invites. Join forums and contribute to social media in your field.

3. There is a libertarian organization called the Institute for Humane Studies (theihs.org) that is infiltrating colleges with the goal of bringing back Western Civilization. Join their organization and use that to make contacts; they are highly connected across the country. Attend their events and apply for their funding program for your graduate degree.

4. Avoid debt as you get your graduate degrees just in case this doesn't work out. This means that you'll need to get a job while going to school.

5. I recommend taking some accounting classes or even getting an accounting minor as a back up plan.

What if your chances of becoming a professor at a large university are extremely small? What if you are in a class of 300 with a 3.0 GPA? You are going to have to bail. In that case, follow these guidelines:

1. First, cheer up a bit as a lot of the classes you took will transfer to a new degree since they usually require general electives. Therefore you didn't completely waste your time.

2. If you are taking history, finance, business administration, or economics, look into transferring to an accounting degree.

3. If you are taking philosophy, finance, business administration, or economics, look into a computer science degree.

4. If you have already graduated and can't find a job that will support a large Catholic family, check out Governor's Western University which is an accredited online college that offers degrees in accounting and I.T. They will accept a lot of your courses which means you can get a new degree in about 2 years. If you go the I.T. route, work on any required certifications while getting your Computer Science degree. This means you have to hit the internet and do your research. Certifications are critical in I.T.

For the rest, use these guidelines:

College

First off, decide if you want to go to college. The most important aspect to consider is cost. Can you pay your way through without going into debt? Student debt can not be discharged via bankruptcy; if you don't pay it off, you will be saddled with it (which includes the garnishment of wages) for the rest of your life.

One trick to lower the cost is to go a year or two to community college and get all of the bull crap prerequisites out of the way. In may cases you can also take the full set of calculus classes, general chemistry, and physics. A lot of times you can go to community college for free. During these 1-2 years you would also work and save up money for University tuition.

Degrees

Here is a list of degrees that will allow you to get a high paying job so that you can support a large Catholic family with a stay-at-home mom:

1. Chemical Engineering. This is the Navy Seal program. My class started with over 300 and we graduated 40. Only try this if you have a MENSA level IQ. However if you get this degree you are set for life.

2. Electrical Engineering. This is a great degree if you concentrate on the Industrial side. What I love about this degree is that you can work anywhere in the US as there is always a powerhouse, refinery, chemical plant, or other manufacturing facility nearby.

3. Mechanical Engineering. This is a good degree that pays well. Concentrate on piping and structures as well as rotating equipment and bearings. You can work in the maintenance department or for an engineering firm.

4. Civil Engineering. Forget about designing bridges, concentrate on building support structures and "site prep" such as drainage (hydrology). Note a lot of men take this degree and make a good living joining the Department of Transportation and supervising road construction and repair.

5. Accounting. If you get this degree, find out the requirements to get a CPA. What I love about this degree is again you can live anywhere in the US. However it is absolutely necessary that you will end up with a CPA.

6. Computer Science. Do some research as there are many flavors, so find out what concentration to take. Also look at certifications and take those online while attending college.

"Big Data", "Machine Learning", and "Blockchain" are currently hot areas.

7. Actuarial Science. Not many people know about this, but it pays very well. Look into it if you are highly introverted.

8. Nursing. Research the field. You will want to go into a specialized area like nurse anesthetist.

9. Ag Science / Food Sciences. If you are from the rural parts, research this degree and find out what concentration to use. This degree is for people who will stay in a rural area. Make sure to check out starting salaries and make sure your degree equates to a readily available high paying job.

10. Internships. Make sure to work an internship during your Junior year summer break. If you are going the engineering route, also work one summer in the oil fields, as this looks great on a resume.

11. Other degrees. I've probably missed some, but a good degree has 2 key attributes: jobs are easy to get and salaries are high. If you do it right in an engineering program, chances are you will have several job offers before you even graduate. Other degrees should come close to matching this.

Tech School

Tech School is a great choice, and if you do it right you will make over $100K per year after putting in your time as an apprentice. Even apprentice pay is decent and making $40K per year is doable. The following is a list of programs to look into:

Electrician. If possible, concentrate on Industrial electrical.

Instrumentation. This cert allows you to work on all of the instruments in modern industrial plants, such as temperature, pressure, flow, and level sensors, as well as analyzers. This skill is in high demand.

Instrument/Electrical. If you can get this combo cert, do it. By combining the two, you are guaranteed a well paying job.

PLC programmer. This cert teaches you to program the control systems in industrial sites. Think of it as a series of relays and timers. This trade is well paid and jobs are plentiful. Make sure the course covers Allen Bradley PLCs (their software is currently RSLogix 500 and RSLogix 5000).

Grand Slam Instrument / Electrical / PLC. Combining all three certs is like printing money.

Rotating Specialist. Here you are trained on large rotary equipment like pumps, turbines, generators, and compressors. You are taught about the shaft, seals, and bearings. This cert will get you a job in the maintenance department of a large industrial site.

Large Engine Mechanic. Concentrate on natural gas engines (popular with large compressors in the oil fields) and large diesel engines. Jobs are plentiful.

Work

I want to begin with two simple rules: 1. All jobs suck (hat tip to Aaron Clarey), and 2. There is no such thing as a career. Your goal is to find work that sucks the least factoring in the pay. Please don't be taken in like goofy feminists and believe that there is such a thing as a career. Tell me the difference between "a job" and "a career". You can't. All jobs suck.

But what about the Entrepreneur programmer making $10K per week working from home, or on the beach? It still sucks due to clients, taxes, and other problems. And most likely you aren't the $10K per week programmer. If you get a good job, it is more like $10K per month, before taxes. Do you still have dreams of changing the world and finding a job you are "passionate" about (please don't ever talk that way.)? Consider that every morning you have to drag your butt out of bed at 6 a.m., get ready, then face the "commute". Then after work, you get to "commute" again, and arrive home brain dead. Steel yourself for life lads, as it is given to you to provide for your family. You might as well make a lot of money doing it.

To begin, I advise that whatever job you take, you go for an all male team to work with. This day and age it is very difficult to find this, however make it your goal. I strongly advise against having a woman boss.

You then have to consider pay level. If you want a large Catholic family, you are going to need $70K per year minimum with benefits. This equates to $35 per hour unless you can get a job that pays for overtime. You aren't going to start out there, but the job field you choose should be able to pay at this level after 5 – 10 years of experience, usually by getting promoted to the supervisor level.

The stand out jobs include most of the engineering fields, though I caution you to concentrate on INDUSTRIAL electrical if you go the electrical engineering route. Most computer chip electrical engineering is done in Asia today, however Industrial electrical is in high demand in the USA.

Another useful degree is accounting, though you MUST get your CPA to go along with it. The accounting degree pays well, and as an added benefit you can set up shop anywhere in the USA. This allows you to locate in a fun location with a good climate and near to a Trad chapel.

I.T. is another great field that pays well. Unfortunately I am not extremely knowledgeable in all of the various fields that fall under I.T., but I do know you can make a lot of money in the field. If you like computers, do some research on pay levels and pick a field that interests you and pays well. One thing I do know is that in addition to a computer science degree you need to take various certifications, so research those also. Luckily most of these are available online.

The medical profession is the perennial money maker, but there is a lot of up-front sacrifice until you are making the big bucks. Evidently there are now high level nursing degrees that pay big bucks, like the assistant to the anesthesiologist (nurse anesthetist). This is an option to consider if you like the medical field, but don't want to blow 12 years of your life becoming a doctor. Do your research on pay levels.

And of course there are lawyers. I strongly recommend that you avoid the legal profession due to the current glut of lawyers (caused by women set adrift due to feminism). The exception is if you can get into a top tier, usually ivy league law school and if you have connections. In that case, a legal profession can be highly lucrative, but again you have to pay your dues up front until the money rolls in.

One option that is now extremely attractive is the trades. The USA is currently run by Vietnam veterans in the trades. Your lights come on when you flip the switch because some Vietnam vet is out at the powerhouse keeping things running during the graveyard shift. And these man have over a million dollars in their retirement plans and their average age is 65 at the time of this writing.

For trades, a really good option is the electrician / instrument man dual trade. If you can throw in PLC programming, you are golden. In order to make it in this field, you should start by getting an associates degree at a tech school, then working on your tools for a few years. Note even as an apprentice, you can easily make $45K per year, which is not bad. After you do the time, you will need to test for your Journeymen's license and become a licensed industrial electrician. After that you have many options:

1. Stay on your tools and move up to foreman or a higher supervisor's position. You can expect high pay and benefits.
2. Study CAD (you can do this before getting your license) and become a designer at an engineering firm. Again expect the big bucks and good benefits.
3. Start your own Industrial firm and run a crew of apprentices. This is probably where you will make the most money, and in fact will likely be considered wealthy.
4. Get your Master's license and start a commercial / residential practice.
5. Get a job at a large industrial site as part of their maintenance crew. Again you will have an opportunity to advance in supervisory roles and you can expect the big bucks and good benefits.

Other trades to consider is diesel mechanic, and then switch to natural gas engines which are ubiquitous in the oil fields;

airplane mechanic, and rotating specialist (pumps, generators, turbines, and compressors) again joining a large industrial company and working in the maintenance department.

Large industrial sites that pay high wages include oil refineries, chemical plants, paper mills, power plants, and mining processing plants. These sites all have large maintenance departments and $100K per year is attainable if you have a good work ethic. With the large retirement of the Vietnam vets upon us I expect wages to only rise from here.

If you can't go to Tech School, then your last option is to start out as unskilled labor in the oil fields. Starting pay is $20/hr., they pay overtime over 40, and you usually get a per diem to pay the rent. If you work hard you can move up to foreman within a year or two, and make the magic $100K. Men working in the Bakken are taking down around $2K per week before tax; however only do this if you are in shape and understand that it is hard work until you can make supervisor. This is not a job for married men, so after a few years you will have to use your experience and resume to make the jump to operations and or maintenance at an industrial site.

Once you have gained about 5 years in your profession, you should consider joining a smaller firm. To start out I recommend working for a large organization. These firms usually have in-house procedures and methods that are very beneficial to learn. Working for them also looks great on a resume.

However you will soon discover that a lot of large companies are run by libtards and most likely you will be subjected to Inclusivitiy and Sensitivity training on an annual basis. Also, more and more companies are switching to a "collaborative" feminine management style where no one is in charge and no one is responsible for screw ups. This usually ends up with low morale and heavy politics. It's pretty depressing. Remember how I started this book talking about communist infiltration and Cultural Marxism? This is not fantasy lads, as you will discover.

Therefore a man should strongly consider jumping ship to a smaller firm that is riding below the radar. Oftentimes these are the places where you can work on an all-male team, as they oftentimes have less than 50 employees, so the EEOC ignores them. For your long term sanity I recommend making this jump and avoiding lifelong Diversity refresher training.

To pull this off while working for the large corporation, keep your eyes open for smaller competitors, service providers that you use, and suppliers. Take your time and do your research. When you have gained about 5 years experience, that will be the time to make your escape.

For certain fields it is also possible to start your own business. This is your definite goal if you get your CPA, and this is also very doable if you are in I.T. If you are in engineering, and have buddies who are in engineering also, it is still possible to do engineering consulting or start your own firm. Note that you will want to create an L.L.C. when you do this to limit your liability. You will also want to work closely with a CPA to stay on the good side of the I.R.S.

In closing, just remember lads: 1. All Jobs Suck, and 2. There is no such thing as a career. Your goal is to make money so that you can support your family and enjoy your life when you are off work. So do your research and make sure you are at least paid a fat salary for the effort.

Section 3: The Ladies

The Preliminaries

In a few cases the men reading this book will skip the first 2 sections and start right here. That is unfortunate (and is guaranteed to lead to failure) because this section is the least important when it comes to slaying the females. Developing Iron Hard frame is the most important; but let us continue, as this section will certainly help you a lot. One word of caution, while my explanation of female nature will certainly help you, none of this will make complete sense until the first time you see your wife holding your baby.

To begin, you will need a model of what a female is. They are dangerous creatures known for their ability to scratch, pinch, and even bite when you really piss them off, so this is important. There's a few ways to think about women so I make it simple and give you two models. Then I'll add in some rules to follow which will keep you out of trouble and help deepen your understanding of female nature.

Imagine a woman who loves the water. In fact, whenever she gets into a swimming pool she is like a little kid splashing around and going wild, having a great time. However there is only one problem – she can't swim.

Now in a particular pool where she wants to splash around there is a 4 foot shallow section and an 8 foot section with an immediate drop off. Another problem with this pool is that there are spiders crawling around outside of it, and she is afraid of spiders. She really wants to splash around in this pool, but she's afraid of the spiders and she knows that when she goes wild in the pool she can easily slip into the 8 foot section and drown. She needs a lifeguard.

Now let me interpret this model: the swimming pool is her emotions, the spiders are threats from the external world, and the lifeguard is her man. What are the attributes that she wants in her lifeguard?

1. He should be decent enough to look at, since she will be in the pool with him.

2. He should be strong and fearless. He may be called upon to deal with the spiders.

3. He should be able to handle her when she is going wild and getting too close to the drop off. (This is key).

4. He should also be fun for the rest of the time, since he will be in charge of her, and she does not want him to be a sour puss.

So the woman gets her lifeguard. First she tests him. She lunges herself at the deep end, after which he responds by grabbing her and throwing her back into the shallow end. She may pout a bit after his response, but deep down she is happy because she knows she can rely on her man to keep her under control. In the real world this is called a shit test, and it is done to see if her man can handle her when she is feeling emotional.

Second she may point to a spider and scream. She is very happy as she watches her man jump from the pool and squash the spider. In the real world this is the woman checking to make sure her man can handle the problems life throws at her.

Third, during normal times in the pool she observes the lifeguard grab a beach ball and start a game with her, which makes her happy. In the real world this is her observing her man take the lead and provide a fun life for her -- planning and executing activities.

Next another model, which is basically the ultimate fantasy of a woman. Imagine a woman promenading down a boulevard with her great looking husband (and we know he has rock solid Frame), her arm wrapped through his elbow as they walk down the boulevard. Along the sides of the boulevard are other women who look jealously at her and her husband. When he is not looking, she turns her head and sticks her tongue out at the other women. The lesson here is that women compete with each other and can strongly hate each other. We will revisit this lesson when I discuss Dread Game, but first we must continue with the basics.

Next, let's go over some rules in life:

1. A woman does not know what she wants until a man gives it to her. The take away for this rule is that women hate making decisions and want their man to decide, or in other words, to lead. Now note she will love worrying about the decision, so don't rush it. This leads to the second rule:

2. A woman is not happy unless she has something to worry about. The takeaway is that unlike men, women are emotional beings. In fact if her life is boring, she will go out of her way to create a situation where she can be emotional. And she is not particular on what type of emotion, as long as it IS emotion: it can make her happy, it can make her sad, or it can make her angry. Women are particularly happy when they are angry as this is a strong emotion. Now you know why women love watching chick flicks.

3. The idea about something is more important than the something. This is confusing, however an example will make it clear. You do not tell your wife you are "taking her skiing". Instead you announce to her that you all will be going on a "romantic ski weekend getaway". The pro who is familiar with the previous laws and topics will announce this a month in

advance to give her time to tell her friends. While chatting about it with her friends she may even be able to work herself into crying over it (maybe she does not know what to wear), which will make her really happy.

4. Women hint. Women don't ask a man directly for things, they hint. The other thing is that they LOVE to hint. Now for a man, hinting is considered rude. If your buddy needed some help and hinted at you to get it, this would be considered an insult. "Hey asshole, you can't ask politely?". If men hinted at other men like women do, there would be fist fights, and I'm not exaggerating.

However women are allowed to hint. This is their nature, and you can't cure it (I have scars dating back to times I tried to cure my late wife of hinting.). It's like men needing to hang with other men sometimes -- it's our nature and there is nothing to "cure". Just be expecting the hints and don't let it bother you. Maintain frame.

This rule comes into play also during what my buddy termed "climbing the ladder". Climbing the ladder is when you go through the rungs of hints to finally get her to tell you the problem.

Female: I can't believe you moved the clothes hamper!
Man: Beth, what's wrong?
Female: What's wrong? The clothes hamper has been moved, that's what's wrong!
Man: Are you going to tell me what's wrong?
Female: This is not important to you?
Man: Of course YOU are important to me, that's why I'm trying to find out what's wrong.
Female: You aren't taking me seriously. It's like last week. You said we would go out for dinner on Friday night, and you forgot!

BINGO! You just climbed the ladder.

5. When women tell you about a problem, they don't want you to solve it. Here you have to draw the line sometimes, if not most of the time, because you are a man and you solve problems. Here's an actual conversation that occurred :

Wife: Oh my gosh, I am so mad. You are not going to believe what (redacted) said/did.

Me: Stop. Are you telling me this because you want me to solve it, or are you telling me this because you want to have a good cry? Because I'm going to tell you how to fix it. I'm going to do that. If that's not what you want, go into the kitchen and call (redacted), and you all can have a good cry about it.

Wife. Pissed off. Might have even stomped her pretty little foot. Goes into kitchen and calls (redacted).

There's another approach I would do that is kind of fun. I can't take credit for this as my buddy is the one who came up with it. Here's what he told me: "Think of it like watching a play. You are the audience and your job is to spot the bad girl, and boo her, and spot the good girl, and cheer her on." It's amazing how well this would work. I suggest using method 1 most of the time, but try out the second method once or twice just for fun.

For your homework, search for "It's not about the nail" on YouTube, which is hilarious. This short video will explain this concept by showing it to you far better than I can do by writing about it. Watch it with your girlfriend also.

6. Women consume emotion. Men provide emotion. This is very, very critical. Note this does not mean you are emotional

yourself. It could mean you piss her off, which she'll like. Passion lads, and we'll get to that.

7. Women seek validation from men. Only give it when it is earned, but remember: thanking her for cooking you a great breakfast means a lot more to her than you would think.

8. Lastly, there is one Law that binds them, one Law to rule them all: Never take crap from a woman.

Next we must discuss the rule about flowers. God made flowers for a reason: to get men out of trouble. For this reason you should rarely give flowers, saving them for an emergency. In some dire situations, to get out of trouble it may be necessary to hit her with the chocolate right after giving her the flowers. Lads, I don't care if you accidentally ran over her new pet kitten with a lawn mower, flowers will get you off the hook. Now in this particular situation you may have to deploy chocolate. After giving her the flowers you would say, "babe, I know I really messed up this time, so I also got you your favorite chocolate bar." It's like it never even happened.

To close this section, no discussion about the nature of women would be complete unless it addresses the age old question: "What do women want?". The answer is one word: Passion. For the younger lads who don't know any better I have this to say: passion does not mean sex. Now for married Catholics passion will often lead to sex, even revenge sex, but passion is not the same thing as sex.

To understand passion, we need to consider the Romance Novel. Now I have never read one, but I've read enough about them in various articles, and seen some chick flicks, so I could probably write one. Here's a synopsis:

A woman is captured by a ruggedly good looking pirate. He brings her aboard his ship as a prisoner. He knows that as a pirate he should rape her and kill her, but due to her beauty he spares her life and makes her his servant girl. Now he does not reveal the reason for sparing her life, but she instinctively knows. She is disorientated by the plethora of emotions raging inside of her: she is attracted by his rugged handsomeness and his choice of wearing a Henley made from fine clothe in a blue that goes with his color palette, which he has matched with some cool pirate boots. She is turned on being made his servant girl and loves the fact that he secretly finds her beautiful. At the same time she is scared about what is going to happen, and she is angry at him for stealing her from her home. The passion is slowly building (well actually at this point she is like a coke head who has done five lines of coke, but go with me here) and over the course of a few weeks of various adventures (ladies who have snuck in to read *The Catholic Red Pill*, to find out more about her adventures a future book will be available on Amazon for only $19.99), the passion builds until she can't take it anymore. They get into a huge fight. He calls her a spoiled bitch and she ends up scratching him. He man-handles her across his lap and gives her a spanking. After this (and by this, I mean Passion) comes sex, love, and happily ever after. I did not say that this was a Catholic book by the way.

One takeaway here is that you should never deny a woman a good fight. Fighting is passionate when done properly. "Properly" means that you obey the rules of no cussing, no cruel comments, and that the man is not allowed to physically harm a woman. Now if you have really pissed her off and she's started scratching, you can grab her and throw her onto the comfy couch (no harm) in self defense. However you will never ever hit a woman. That is unacceptable for a man. Note that this does not exclude giving her a spanking from time to time. That's allowable, and don't be surprised when she goes out of her way to get one. One other advantage of fighting is that it allows both sides to address problems and it prevents grudge holding.

Now there is no relationship that can maintain passion 24/7, so actually the more important question is "What is the second thing that women want?". The answer is, to be important to you. To be a complement to your life. This leads to another rule about fighting: if in doubt about who is wrong and who is right, always go with the fight over the apology. If it turns out you were right, you passed her test and even gave her some passion. If it ends up that you were wrong, you then apologize. By apologizing you show that she is important to you, maybe even important enough to go out and get some flowers.

I need to stress this because it is important for a long term relationship like marriage. A woman observes your actions and interprets them as to whether she is important to you or not. Telling her you will do something, and then not doing it shows that she is not important. This is bad. However, you do have to establish a balance. Many men…. MOST men will put their girlfriend on a pedestal and run around to her beck and call: "What can I do for me Lady?". This is actually worse than the man who sometimes forgets to do something, as at least he is a challenge. You have to find the proper balance. I'd say one rule is to always keep your word. If you say you will do something, then a man always honors his word. Do it. Second, you have to determine if she is giving you a shit test, which I will discuss later. If she's testing you, then the answer is usually to tell her no.

How to Get the Girls

It all starts with solid frame. Do not attempt to approach the ladies until you have made good progress on developing solid frame. For some men this may be possible after only a month, for others it might take a year. If you are fifty pounds over weight, eat crap, have zero upper body strength, live with your parents, have no future prospects, have no hobbies, and spend all your time playing video games, don't even think about women. It's going to take you a year to get to that point.

Attraction vs. Provision

To begin I have to correct an error that 90% of men make: stressing provision over attraction. The providers often find out that they have been dumped by their girlfriend when they see her ride by on the back of some dude's motorcycle. Don't make this mistake.

This binary of Attraction vs. Provision is probably the most important thing to know if you want to have solid Game. You really need to get this. So what do I mean by attraction vs. provision? Let me go over two actual field reports, because some of you will be stuck on stupid and not get this. Note, this is not theory, this is how it went down:

<u>Report 1:</u> A PUA YouTube channel set up a hidden camera in a sports bar / restaurant kind of place. They sent in the first guy, a bad boy player who had zero intimidation and looked the part. He approached a table of women and started chatting them up. They ate it up, and he threw in some heavy sexual innuendo, which the girls enjoyed. They were laughing and having fun with him. Heck, at times there wasn't even innuendo. He went out of his way to push being an asshole just to prove the point – the girls played along and had a good time. Then he excused

himself and left, but it was pretty obvious he could have scored some fornication if he wanted.

Next they sent in a second guy, who we will call the Dentist, because that's what he claimed to be. He was tall, good looking, and was dressed well, but conservative. He was also confident and approached the same table. In this case he used polite language. The girls liked him, but the vibe was obviously different. Then he slipped in one naughty joke, which was no where near half as bad as what the previous bad boy was saying. The girls got offended. "You shouldn't talk like that, it's rude". This from women who themselves had been saying much worse only a few minutes previously.

At this point they ended the experiment, brought back the bad boy, and explained to the girls what they were doing. They then questioned them. The girls said that they were attracted to the first man, but considered the second man as "boyfriend material". This is why they got offended, because when he cracked his joke, it ruined their "boyfriend" impression of him.

Now at this point the provider simps are cheering. "See, we're right. I'll treat her like "me Lady", and I'll be her boyfriend!". You're missing a few things. Did you miss where they said they were ATTRACTED to the first man? <u>Do you want a girlfriend and then wife who is not attracted to you?</u> Think about that one long and hard. Oh, and you forgot I said there were TWO field reports.

<u>Report 2:</u> This report covers the circumstances around a divorce. A provider simp got married. He followed all of the rules. He was a good provider with a great job who dutifully took care of his wife and went out of his way to please "me Lady". There was one problem with his marriage: his bedroom was dead. Sex was rare, and when it happened, she just laid there. When he whined to her about it, she told him that sex

was not a big deal to her, and that she never enjoyed it. Then he found the pictures.

In their closet she kept a box of pictures, including from her college days. To say that she had been wild is an understatement as there was a picture of her with TWO men, and that's as far as I'll go with that. It turns out she actually liked having sex, just not with him. Instead she liked Frat boys who probably ended up as underpaid motorcycle mechanics. He didn't know what to do, and couldn't handle it, so they ended up divorced. Obviously neither were Catholic.

So what is a Catholic man to do? Should he talk crudely to women? Should he fornicate? No. A Catholic man should read *The Catholic Redpill* where the author has picked out the important empirical observations, stripped them of sin and fornication, added in the Catholic Virtue, and explains to you how to attract women in a moral way (which I'll be getting to), AND end up with a good marriage. Furthermore, the goal is BOTH: Attraction AND Provision; however it changes with time. When you first approach, it is 100% attraction. When you are dating, it is 90% attraction. Married, no kids? 80% attraction. Married, with kids? 50% attraction. That is your answer.

I'll continue by discussing what is meant by provision and how men try to sell themselves as good providers. Men will oftentimes feel the need to discuss their ability to provide for a girl. They'll discuss their education and their job or job prospects. They will dress very conservatively and constantly do favors for her. Another prominent feature for these men is that they will blow up her phone with text messages and call her everyday -- when they are not busy liking her Facebook posts. And that's it.

Most of the time the girl will end up treating such a man as her gay friend or her girlfriend. She'll use him to do chores for her (can you come over and help me move?) or call him on the phone when she is sad to have a good cry, just like she does with her girlfriends. The Provider Simp thinks he is doing good because he has not been outright rejected. He believes eventually she will come to her senses and realize what a great guy he is. What he doesn't realize is that he bores her and that he has been stuck in the Friend Zone – forever. A worse outcome is if they end up married. We'll discuss fixing a marriage if you have been living like a provider simp in a later section. For now we are still on meeting hot little Trad girls.

The topic of the Friend Zone is very critical, so I've dedicated a later section to discuss it, but only after we finish talking about female nature, as well as attraction vs. provision. Don't worry, I'll give you advise on what to do if you have been friend zoned later, but for now let's continue with the preliminaries:

What is attraction, or to ask a better question: What are women attracted to? One word, Testosterone. Now since she won't be checking your T levels, I need to be more specific. Women are attracted to displays and signs of high testosterone. What are those signs?

1. The V shape. Broad shoulders (upright rows and shoulder flies lads), broad back, low percent body fat, and decent abs.

2. Facial hair. The stubble / 5 o'clock shadow is killer.

3. Competence. Competence comes from the practice of various skills, etc...., which you will gain when you develop your intellectual side, hobbies, skills, and activities.

4. Confidence. Develops as you grow your competency level. This also comes about when you strengthen the emotional side

of Frame, and have tried and failed (learn or lose lads) at various things, only to try again and succeed. Getting the green horn wiped out of you by an all-male work crew also builds confidence.

5. Boldness. Add up Competence, Confidence, some level of fighting ability, and a mastery of Frame in general and you will develop boldness.

6. Open Body Language. This is when your body language is congruent with all that you have achieved. What does open body language LOOK like? Imagine walking somewhere with an unzipped coat, hands in the pockets, and your head held high, not looking at the ground. You're feeling real positive and strong. You'll have the coat spread open and you'll have good posture. You'll be open to the world because you feel good. That is an example of Open Body Language.

Does all of this sound familiar? I wasn't kidding when I said developing Frame was the most important thing you could do to attract the females.

Finally there is one more important topic to discuss. In Red Pill literature men often discuss a change in mindset that comes about as you develop Solid Frame. If you follow the program for developing the emotional side of frame, you'll learn about mindset, but for this section I'll just discuss this change. Various aspects of the change have been described in various ways:

1. You are your own mental point of origin. You are strong spiritually (and here, the Spiritual Side of Frame really stands out), mentally, and intellectually. Therefore you are well grounded and run your own life.

2. You are your own interior point of reference. Again you have developed spiritually and have been working on the virtues. Therefore you have a well developed conscience and more times than not choose the right course of action.

3. Self amusement / amused mastery. You enjoy life and do things that make you happy. If a girl rejects you, or shit tests you, you find that amusing while giving her a knowing smirk. You never whine or get butt hurt.

4. ZFG. Zero Fucks Given (that's what it stands for). If a girl rejects you, you really don't care. You'll just game another one.

5. Developing the Best Version of Yourself. Here the virtue of Magnanimity stands out. You feel life is beautiful and a blessing, and you want to make the most of it.

6. Abundance Mindset. You have Solid Frame and view the world as full of opportunity. You know where you are going with your job, hobbies, and friends, and you know that there are plenty of cute Trad girls out there to game.

If you follow the program in the beginning of this book and develop strong frame, you will undergo this mindset shift. Trust me, women will pick up on it and this boosts their attraction level. If I have to sum up what this means, I say what has happened is that you have developed the habit of the Virtue of Magnanimity.

<u>Game</u>

To begin, I'm making some assumptions as follows:

1. You have developed strong frame, or at least you have made huge progress. You are saying to yourself: "Wow, this book really works. Life has gotten so much better."

2. You have been working on the Virtue of Magnanimity, and you at least "get it".

3. You are active in at least a few hobbies. If you now ride around on a motorcycle, give yourself extra credit.

4. You have been working on the skills I mentioned in the previous section of the book.

5. You see that you are becoming more competent. If your buddy asked you to help out with some manly activity, you'd confidently head over to his house with your toolbox, ready to help out.

6. You have a plan and/or are executing a plan that will end up with you getting a good job that will allow you to support a large Catholic family. DO NOT start hunting female until you reach this level. You are being dishonest trying to get a woman if you have no ability to support her and your future kids, or are at least working on that seriously (if you are young).

Well, to be honest I'm surprised you don't already have a girlfriend. But perhaps no one has ever really explained to you the process, and this is that last step you need to make. Don't worry, we'll take care of you.

Next, <u>it is important going in that you set high standards.</u> You are now a great catch (see the list above – that's a good catch), so don't settle for low quality. Here's what you are after:

1. She is Catholic. Conservative Catholic at the minimum, but you really want a Traditional Catholic.

2. She's a virgin. If you are older, and in this day and age, perhaps you can go with a girl that messed up early, then returned to Christ (e.g. she screwed up in high school). This is probably acceptable if she has been a good Catholic for awhile <u>and</u> you are older so it's slim pickings, but it's not optimal. Note I really hesitate in saying this is ok, but it is marginally acceptable if you are late to the party and you have high confidence that she's legit and not looking for captain save-a-ho.

Before we progress to "3", I want to spend a few paragraphs to warn you about a common trap in this day-and-age via an "example". We will talk about Chris and Beth.

Chris was a 37 year old introvert "Delta" when he found this book: the quiet nice guy that people tend to like. He has excelled at I.T. and takes down the six figs. He finds the book and goes hard core. After a year he's shed 30 lbs. while adding 10 lbs. of muscle, and he's up for testing at his next level of Jui Jitsu. When he leaves the house he's dressed well, and oftentimes takes his motorcycle to work. He has learned to swing dance and spends weekends hunting and fishing. At this point, at age 38, he decides he's ready for a wife.

Beth became sexually active at 17, and never quit – even attending spring break partying in Daytona and Cancun. She's been so promiscuous that she has lost count – it's probably pushing 100. At age 28 she notices that male attention levels are starting to decrease and she decides it's time to lock down a man. She also remembers she was kind of Catholic as a kid and has heard about how nice church going Catholics are. So she starts going to Mass and cuts down somewhat on her fornication. She also buys feminine clothes and creates a profile on Catholic Match which contains a lot of discussion of how important her "Faith" is to her.

This sounds like the script from a Hallmark girly chick flick where the wayward girl is finally saved by her white knight. Except this story won't have a happy ending.

Chris and Beth get married. And then the problems start for these reasons:

a. Beth is not truly a penitent. If she were, she would realize the horror of her life and do penance in a convent for the rest of her life. Barring that, all she is doing is looking for a chump to lock down.

b. While Chris has the benefit of this book and does indeed have strong frame, he's not experienced, and ALL men fall into the "drunk captain" (discussed later) scenario from time to time. Which is a problem because,

c. Beth can no longer emotionally bond with a man. As long as Chris is staying strong and leading, he can PROBABLY keep her straight, but once he slackens, she'll get hurt and immediately start texting with her ex "boyfriends". Eventually she will cheat. Another problem with a "party girl" is that they oftentimes see children as a burden that locks them down. They make horrible mothers and home makers.

For the late arriver, say over 35, my advice is to filter your dating search app for widows only. Another option is to try to find a local late-bloomer wallflower type girl whom you are familiar with her background. Note if you can't get a good looking widow chances are you will have to lower your physical standards somewhat (though you can work on improving her later) or your personality match standards (the wallflower might bore you, but you get a nice home life and your kids will get a good mom – not a bad deal). This is a tough one, so you might end up living a life as a single man, though I think as you get older there will be more widows to choose from.

One more thing, do not date a single mom (besides a widow). Don't do it.

3. Long hair.

4. Thin.

5. She's a good cook. She even brags about it. This is critical, and many young men don't even think about it. Imagine coming home from work every night and having to eat something with the consistency and taste of the cardboard box it came out of. This is your dinner and this is what you'll be eating for the next 50 years every day of your miserable life. This one is critical lads.

6. Feminine attire and attributes.

7. She was raised in a traditional intact family.

8. She has a good relationship with her Dad whom she loves.

These are the standards lads. You are a good catch, so insist on a quality girl. And yes they are available in Trad Catholic circles.

Next I will talk about a particular Game mindset, which has two important attributes. Note that this is in addition to the positive mindset you developed when you worked on the Emotional Side of Frame and the mindset shift you experienced as Magnanimity grew within you:

1. Zero intimidation. You don't care if you are rejected, that's her huge loss. Girls don't intimidate you. Here's an easy way to gain zero intimidation (besides the practice I go over below): Think of rejection as being hit by a water balloon. Now normally you don't want to get hit with one, but at the end of the day it is no big deal. However by risking getting hit by said balloon, you open up huge opportunities to find a pot of gold. Think of it that way.

2. You are the buyer, not the seller. So many men make the mistake of selling themselves, again, being the provider. You aren't selling anything. You are the buyer and you are evaluating what you will "buy".

I want to delve a little deeper into being a buyer. If you approach a girl and initiate contact, aren't you selling? And if you've spent months working on solid frame, isn't that developing something to sell? This sounds like a contradiction. No and no.

First, imagine that you want to buy a laptop. Does the dude from Walmart's electronics department show up at your house with a van? "Hey, I heard you want to buy a new laptop, come on outside and I'll show you all the models I have brought with me in my van." Of course not. Even though in this case you are definitely the buyer, you will be the one that initiates contact with the electronics dude so that you can check out the merchandise. This is the same thing as having the buyer mindset when it comes to women.

Second, while developing Solid Frame has the benefit of attracting the ladies, and this is a great benefit we want to be cognizant about, this is NOT the reason to develop Frame. No, the motivation to develop Solid Frame is this: YOU WANT TO BE A MAN.

With this Game mindset in place, it is now time for approach. But before the Game, it is important to put in the practice. So how do you practice approach?

I'm going with the assumption that you are a complete chicken and turn pale just thinking about talking to a woman. Let me cheer you up: I can say with complete confidence that you are definitely NOT a fag. Fags easily chat up women. So there's that. Now I'm going to take a worst case scenario. If you are somewhat better than this, then just adjust the practice routine I'm laying out.

First you have to take a small step and fortunately there's a real easy way to do this: the convenience store. Pick up something at the store, and approach the counter with your wallet already in your hand. As you walk up to the counter, look the check-out girl in the eye, and say this: "How's it going?". Then I want you to naturally shift your gaze to your wallet and take out your debit card, so you've safely ended contact. And that's it. Do this at different stores for a week until it just becomes natural.

Congratulations, you are now farther along than before. At least you can now talk to a girl, even if it's only for a few seconds. For the next phase, skip the wallet trick. Say, "Hey, how's it going" and maintain contact. Don't keep staring at her, keep it natural with a smile, but most likely she'll say, "Fine, how about you?". You respond anyway you want, maybe "It's going pretty good. I'm looking forward to getting home though. Been a long day.". Most likely she may say something else, but she has to check you out so there's an end to this torture. Do this for a week.

Congratulations, you are now conversing with females. I didn't think you had it in you, good job. For the following week, look to develop natural conversation. If it's a short, "How's it going" kind of deal, don't sweat it and don't force it. The key is to keep it natural. However if the girl is feeling chatty, chat away. Tell her about the crazy ride you had getting to her store on your motorcycle. Talk to her about the cool camping trip you just went on, or the great mountain biking adventure. However, don't push it, let it flow, and keep it natural. Don't force the situation. When it ends, it ends and wish her a good day. Also, and this is key, during these sessions make sure you are confidently making eye contact. One final thing, don't worry if you screw it up and say something stupid. That's the whole point of this practice, it doesn't count. Keep at it until you easily converse with the females while remaining authentic (remember your Solid Frame and cool hobbies?).

Well dude, you are there, and look at the progress you have made in only a few weeks time. However, there's the final exam left to do, and then it's on to the playing field. The final exam is practicing "the neg". What is the neg you might ask? Negging is teasing the girl. Done right, it's a complement wrapped in an insult. As always, there are some preliminaries to discuss:

1. Negging is NEVER cruel. "Man are you a fat whale!" is not negging. Never be cruel.

2. Remember the escape hatch to get out of the neg: You smile at her while you say, "I'm just messing with you.". Learn that one well.

Here's a few examples to give you an idea what negging looks like:

1. You are in a Subway store, and the girl is flying making your sandwich. She should be competing in the Subway Olympics she's so quick. You give her an impatient look and say, "You know, you need to pick up the pace. I need to get somewhere.". She looks up somewhat confused, and then you give her the smile and say, "I'm just messing with you, you are a real pro."

2. You are in a restaurant, and the waitress comes up and starts with "Welcome to Blakely's on the Thames, how's your day going?". You give her an almost mean look and say, "It's going like crap, and thanks for reminding me how bad it is.". This will throw her off, then out comes the smile: "I'm just messing with you, I'm doing great. I'll start off with a Coke Zero.".

3. Here's an easy one. You go into the old standby convenience store and approach the counter. You pause to look at the girls fingernails, which have some sort of weird color, look at her with some disapproval and say, "I don't know about that fingernail polish.". Then you pull out the escape, giving her that grin: "I'm just messing with you. How's your day been going?".

4. You're in a restaurant and the waitress drops a plate making a loud noise. The asshole applauds or says, "Good job". Congrats, you were cruel and you made her feel like crap. No, the next time you interact you say, "I could say something, but I decided not to.". Then out comes the ole grin and you say, "I'm just messing with you. Don't worry about it.", again grinning and having fun with it.

5. Here's a good one that is not technically a neg. It's more "messing with a girl", but you can count it as a neg for the final exam. You walk into the ole convenience store and observe that the girl is not smiling. When you approach the counter you look her in the eye and say, "smile, it's not that bad." She will

inevitably smile after that comment. Chat her up a little, and that's it.

Here's the deal lads. If you pull off a few negs, you have graduated. Your intimidation level is now down to an acceptable level. Now it's time to run Game.

Yes, you guessed it, I have to discuss 3 things with you to make sure you are prepared:

1. Girl's have 10 times the social awareness than men. Women are constantly pinging off the environment and they can read you like a book. This is why the Omegas and other people with weak frame are so quickly rejected or Friend Zoned. No problem, you have strong frame.

2. There's no such thing as a pick up line. Want a pick up line? How about, "Hi, my name is Bill.". There you go. Forget about the stupid pick up line and don't go looking for a list of them, or worse, practicing pick up lines. That is weak. Instead, be authentic. You've just been doing it for weeks during practice, so just keep doing what you've been doing.

Still don't believe me that there is no such thing as a pick up line? How about this: Do you think it is possible to pick up a girl by telling her you are a cockroach? I'm not saying that this will definitely work, or even that it will work half the time, but be honest when I ask you if this might actually work once in awhile. Here's how it would go down:

Man: Hi, I'm a cockroach. (Said with a grin, having a good time.)

Woman: What? You are so weird.

Man: I'm just messing with you. Be real.

Woman: Yeah, but that's still weird.

Man: You're being immature, you need to grow up.

Woman: What? I can't believe you said that (notice you are feeding her emotion).

Man: Didn't I just get done saying I was messing with you? Hi, I'm Bill.

Would this actually work, even if rarely? Forget about a pick up line, it's a waste of time. Solid Frame is all that you need.

Why are pick up lines unnecessary? Go back and review what went down during Cockroach Game (and please don't try this and expect it to work – unless you just want to do it and have some fun.). First, you definitely approached. Second you said something completely crazy. So how would you rate the intimidation level? Somewhere around zero.

Next you pulled an escape, but it didn't work at first. So you went with an old stand by (I'll go more into depth on this later) and pissed her off. Now this is key. You've pissed her off and fed her emotions. Trust me at this point she has forgotten about the cockroach opener because her emotion hamster wheel is really spinning. But it gets even better. <u>Where is 100% of her attention focused?</u> On you. This is key. The goal for approach, even Sigma approach, is to get her to focus on YOU. Let's continue with the final preparatory point.

3. Remember that during conversation and especially during approach, eye contact is critical.

We are finally here: approach. There are 4 ways to approach. 2 are wrong, which means most men do it, one is correct, and the final one works, but is rare. I just mention it to be complete.

1. The Omega "approach". The guy who has ZERO frame and nothing going on in his life. He will get close to the girl without making any attempt to talk to her. When they make eye contact, he quickly looks away, usually down. His hope is that she will notice him and start the conversation. Do I even need to explain how bad this is? Do you know what she is thinking? It's a "creep out". She's imagining you stuffing her dead mutilated body into the trunk of your car. Or the shrine you have of her on your wall with all the pictures of her you secretly took. Don't ever, ever do this. Did you even read the first sections of this book?

2. The Common Approach. 90% of men who actually do approach will try this route. Here the goal of the man is to talk with the girl without letting her know that he is interested in her. What? Yeah, he's trying to talk with her without letting on that he likes her. This is dripping with weakness. And guess what? Women have 10 times the social awareness than this poor schlep, so she already knows he's interested. Why pull some bull crap like this when she already knows you are interested? Why? – Fear of rejection; in other words, intimidation. In fact, deep down she will have some level of disgust by this approach. Now this sometimes does work. If you are really good looking she will flirt heavily with you to help you along. But man, you are starting things off on the wrong foot and this is weak. Don't do this.

A quick aside. The ladies who have snuck into *The Catholic Red Pill* book because of their feminine wiles have just said to themselves: "Oh my gosh, this is so true. They are so obvious when they do this". Now back to the book.

3. The Bold Approach. You make eye contact, walk up to her and say, "You really look great. My name is Bill." Or you throw in a neg: You approach, but notice her shoes in an obvious way. "You really look great, but I don't know about those shoes." Pause. Grin. "I'm just messing with you. My name is Bill, and you really are pretty." She's great looking. She knows you are interested. Go up and talk to her. You have a romantic interest in her, and that's why you are talking with her. Zero intimidation. ZFG. Self Amusement. Solid Frame. It's all there and that's what you go with. Very high success rate, and it it doesn't work, her huge loss. You are the one with Solid Frame.

Here is a true story about a man who is called the Natural Alpha. He was born this way and probably never had an awkward moment with a woman in his life (the son of a gun). He's still my buddy today. Anyhow, we'd be in an office setting and be talking. He'd stop talking and stare hard over my shoulder (and I knew what this meant.). Sure enough a hot looking woman was walking our way. He'd break out into a grin and when she got close, he'd say something like, "Well look at you. How's your day going?". She'd grin and start chatting. They'd chat, and then when she left, she'd be shaking her tail at him. Pretty amazing.

4. Sigma Approach. In case you don't know what a Sigma is, he is an introverted Alpha. Think James Bond. He has iron hard frame. He definitely has magnanimity, and is his own mental point of origin. He is interested in what he is interested in and wouldn't think about pandering to a woman.
At a party, he notices a hot chick in the distance. Since she is a female who constantly pings off of her environment, especially at social situations, she will eventually scan the crowd. The Sigma waits for this, then makes hard eye contact with her. It almost conveys "Danger. You might not survive this encounter.", but in a James Bond kind of way. He does live a

dangerous life after all, where bullets often fly. After freezing her with the eye contact, he gives her a knowing smirk that conveys "Caught you. You were checking ME out.". He maintains eye contact until she is forced to look away, embarrassed (feeding her emotion), and then he completely ignores her, never looking at her again. She no longer exists. He's having interesting conversations with his buddies. Lads, this actually works and is amazing when you can pull it off. The girl goes completely nuts. She will try to get his attention. She will "accidentally" bump into him. She'll embarrass herself. When this goes down right, the girl loses control and approaches HIM.

By the way, if a girl ever "accidentally" bumps into you, you immediately say loudly, "Well that was incredibly rude." (which is a neg). When she whips around (you just fed her emotions), out comes the grin, and well, you know what to do. You escape the neg, then introduce yourself, throwing in a complement how you like Trad women like her that come to parties wearing an apron and heels.

A word of caution. Don't be a chicken cluck and use the Sigma approach as an excuse to get out of the Bold approach. "Well I have solid frame, so I'm probably a Sigma. This is my approach.". That's excuse making because you are a chicken cluck. As a rule, go ahead and give this a try just to have some fun, but ONLY after you have been doing bold approach for some time.

And that's it. That's approach and its the least important part of Game, though this is what scares men the most. Next you have to lock down your romantic interest, at least for the evaluation phase. I'll talk about personality match later; for now, you are entering evaluation.

A quick aside about female flirting. Suppose you see a girl that's good looking, and she flirts with you. What should you do? First, what does flirting look like? The classic is for her to try to catch your eye, make quick eye contact, then look away as if embarrassed. What should you do? If you don't immediately approach, you are a chicken cluck, because this is a 100% home run. Do it. Now back to what happens after the approach.

To begin, remember this mindset (which also applies to escaping the Friend Zone): She's either a romantic interest, or you aren't interested. And remember, you are the buyer. You aren't sold yet.

You've made your approach and now have 100% of her focus. At this point, you should shift into natural, easy going conversation that is not forced. Think about the girl evaluating the lifeguard. Keep it fun and relaxed. Also, use some "push-pull". Throw in some negs, then switch back to conversation which will keep her off balanced and make you a challenge. As a general rule you should let her do 70% of the talking. Think of her as a squirrel and you are feeding her nuts of conversation topics. Have you ever watched a squirrel working on a nut? Takes them a long time. And since she will be nervous in the presence of your Solid Frame, she will be more talkative than usual, which is fine.

Since you have Solid Frame, are skilled, and have interesting hobbies and abilities, you should have a variety of things to talk about. I need to point out that this is where developing the Intellectual side of Frame also helps out. One important point, never brag. Bragging is always weak; it's you trying to prove yourself and "earn" her approval. Don't do this. Trust me, if you are authentic, it will naturally come out that you are a good catch. And I want to stress that word: naturally.

Here, you are leading with attraction, and that is key. Since your Body side of Frame is tip top, you will also be hitting her with physical attraction. Forget about provision. It may come out, it might not. Think of provision as just the cherry on top of a large delicious Sundae of attraction.

Man: "Well, I have to go, I have to go to work in the morning."

Woman: "Oh, too bad. Where do you work?"

Man: (unintentional, just responding to a question naturally) "I work at Megabucks Inc. as the I.T. Manager. It's a cool job."

And that's it for provision, if it even comes up at all.

In general, it should be YOU that breaks off contact. Maybe you do have to leave. Maybe you have been meaning to talk to a buddy that you haven't seen in awhile. So break off contact, but again, natural is the key. Don't force it, but at the same time don't prolong a conversation in a needy way. Breaking off interaction is a most excellent way to show you are not needy. If she is the one who has to run, don't sweat it, this is not critical, just preferred.

Now remember, she is your romantic interest, so this is critical -- pay attention: Establish the date, particularly time and place.

Man: "I have to get going, but this has been great. I want to take you out for a coffee sometime, when are you available?". Set the time, place, and date, and give her your contact info, and get hers. Then you can leave, mission accomplished. When you break contact there should be zero doubt that you have her locked down. If she instead tells you that she has a boyfriend, just say, "Well, when you get tired of him, look me up, I'd like to take you out sometime." Offer her your phone number. Maybe she'll take it, maybe not – don't force it. If she balks some other way, just say, "Well, when you figure out your schedule, get in touch with me because I'd like to take you out some time." Give her your number and then leave. Again you now know where you stand, and you have left the door open in a bold way.

Until a day before date time, leave her alone. Do not blow up her phone. Don't contact her at all. If SHE initiates contact, respond, keep it pleasant, and keep it short. You can end with "see you on Saturday" if you want, but don't pile on the "I'm so excited about Saturday" or anything needy like that. <u>Avoid demonstrating a fear of losing her.</u> You have plenty of options because you are a great catch. You did the work and constructed a Solid Frame.

If you haven't heard from her, send her a short message the day before confirming she's good for the date. It's just logistics. Keep it short and save the conversation for the face-to-face interaction.

Now a quick aside on what to do if she flakes, that is, balks or calls off the date. Keep it pleasant; don't get butt hurt. Sometimes things actually do come up that are unplanned, but in general she should be going out of her way to see you. If not? fine, keep it pleasant. However the same rules apply as you'll see in escaping the Friend Zone. Keep it short. Ask her out only one more time (she only gets two chances), and never initiate contact after a flake beyond "let me know when you get it figured out", unless you have hard proof her reason for canceling is legit, and I mean hard proof: she sends a picture of her arm in a cast. Don't make an excuse to be needy.

So she's balking. You say, "ok, but if you get your schedule sorted out, give me a call, I'd like to take you out." Then cut off contact. Next time she calls, ask her out. That's her second chance. After that, keep it short and pleasant, but now it is up to her to tell you she wants to go out. That's the aside for a flake out.

Now the date. In general, a date should be fun and relaxed. You as the man should lead. You open her car door when she gets out, and you open it when she gets in. You hold the door to the coffee shop. If you needed reservations, you took care of it like a man. You select the table and lead her to it (you walk in front). You scoot her chair in for her. You own your shit, as the saying goes. During the fun and relaxed date you have natural conversation, with her talking 70% of the time. You never brag, but you try to keep the topics either on her life (most of the time) and your hobbies and abilities. Forget about provision, trust me, she'll bring it up.

She's a woman, and she will eventually get curious to know if you can provide for her, but don't be surprised if that doesn't come until much later. For now, she's enjoying being in your frame and having fun.

This brings up a good mindset for any interaction with a romantic interest, especially on dates. You allow her to experience your Frame. This is the reason she agreed to a date, she enjoyed the little taste she got of your Frame and she wants more. You never, ever enter into her Frame. You are the Lifeguard, you are the man, so you must maintain your Frame. You also look for opportunities to lead, but this should never be artificial or forced, as that is weak. Again the key word is natural; and it should be natural if you have Strong Frame.

At the end of the date, you tell her on the ride back you had a great time and you want to take her out again sometime. When she says she also had a great time, tell her you'll think something up and give her a call. Don't ask her what she wants to do, this is an opportunity to take charge and lead, which you will do when you call her in a few days. So you would say,

"This has been fun, I'd like to take you out again sometime, maybe next weekend. When are you available?". When she agrees, you say, "Great. I'll figure something out then call you with the details.".

By the way, this is a good time for me to point out to avoid being robotic. If you are having a natural conversation and end up making a definite, detailed date (time and place), that's fine, though not optimal. Don't be thinking: "The book said to wait a few days, so must avoid, must avoid. Don't set the place. Don't set the place.". Use common sense. The key principles are authentic and natural. NATURALLY put her off a few days if possible. This shows you are not a needy simp. This really needs to be stressed: I'm not giving you the recipe or the cheat codes, I'm trying to teach you to avoid being needy and avoid being the "seller" instead of the buyer.

Make sure you know where you stand after the date. She'll probably say yes, but if she balks, same rules apply, and I won't repeat them. Give her room to build attraction. The response would be along the lines of "alright, when you figure out your schedule, give me a call because I'd like to take you out.". Then drop it. Now in this case, you will not be the one to initiate contact because there's no date to set up. She is the one who balked, so she is the one who has to call.

Assuming she agreed to the next date, you'll wait a few days, then give her a call, again keeping it short. Do not repeat with the same date. During the call set time and place, then end the call soon afterward. Again, you definitely want to know where you stand. Now we get to the end of this date.

Drive her home and then walk her to her door; and assuming you are going on another date, now is the time for the hand kiss, which no man knows how to do anymore. If I could accomplish just one thing with this book, it would be to teach men how to properly kiss a woman's hand, and it is deadly. So here goes:

When you reach the door, you extend your arm and hand. Your hand should be at about her chin level, just a touch lower. The hand is bent sharply at a 90 degree angle, fingers pointing to your left, if you are using your right hand. Use common sense, give her some room so she can put her hand on yours without it being awkward. She should naturally catch on, but if not, look down at her hand and say loudly, "ahem". She should then place her hand on top of your hand, and this is where men screw it up. You absolutely do not grab her hand. In fact, your hand doesn't move. You then make hard eye contact, and slowly bring her hand to your lips (and I mean it, go slow), basically with your arm bending at the elbow. You are forcing her to follow since you aren't holding her hand, never breaking eye contact. You then kiss her hand softly, then slowly return to the starting position, all the while making eye contact. At this point she will be frozen. I guarantee it she'll be in a trance. You then crack a bad boy smirk and then straighten out your hand abruptly (fingers now pointing at her) which will cause her hand to drop, which will snap her out of it and make her a little embarrassed (feeding her emotion lads, and this definitely qualifies as passion).

Then tell her she had better get inside since you both are good Catholics, watch her safely enter her house, then leave.

Now let's go over escaping the Friend Zone by applying what you have learned in these previous sections.

Escaping the Friend Zone

Before you put these methods to escape the Friend Zone into practice, it is important to have the right mind set:

1. Women and men can never be friends.

2. As a man, a woman is either a romantic interest, or no interest.

3. This particular female is high quality. That is why you entered into her orbit (and frame) to begin with. Don't forget your initial impression that she's a great catch – your gut feel is probably correct.

4. Therefore, ALL interactions with this female will be pleasant. She's a quality girl.

5. The reason you are in the Friend Zone is 100% your fault. You were a pussy. You entered her frame and became her gay friend and her emotional tampon to soak up her tears. That's ALL on you. However, that is now gone, a mistake. And remember the rule on mistakes: Learn or Lose. You owned this mistake, and you fixed it.

6. If at any time you slip up and return to simping, let these words keep ringing in your brain: "I'm acting like her gay friend.". Pick yourself up, and improve.

Now escaping the Friend Zone can be a very complicated problem, e.g. are you forced to meet her in person, or does she call up to have a good cry? Therefore I'll give you the general outline, and then discuss some specific situations:

1. Cut off all contact.

2. Never initiate contact, unless you have definite plans for a date, in which case a short confirmation message a day before is acceptable.

3. Always cut contact she has initiated short. However, keep it pleasant: "It's great to hear from you, but I'm busy right now. Catch up with me later."

4. If you have improved in developing Solid Frame, from that point on always assume that when she initiates contact, she wants to go out on a date.

5. Use the word "Date". For example, "It's great to hear from you. I want to take you out on a coffee date sometime, what's your schedule look like this week?".

6. You will invite her out on a date two times. During one of these invitations, she has to respond with a definite yes, and you must set the specifics: Date, Time, and Place.

7. If you don't establish Date, Time, and Place, then that is a strike. After two strikes, you will never ask her out again. She will have to do that.

8. Note a girl is never going to ask you out on a date – she will hint. Hinting is acceptable. For example, let us say you had two failed date invitations, and a month goes by. She has contacted you off-and-on (which you always cut short and don't bring up a date), and now this time she throws out a hint: "You know, we never could schedule that coffee because of my crazy schedule. That would have been nice.". That's acceptable, and you would reply, "Yeah, that would be great. What's your schedule look like now? I'd like to take you out on a coffee date.".

Now let's go over some particular situations:

1. Easy Case. Basically all of your comms are done electronically via text, email, and other messages. Since as part of the program you know that incessant texting is gay, this should be automatic. Let her initiate contact, and cut if off short. You are busy. You are starting on a total work out program (this book), and you'll be snowed under for a few months. It's great hearing from you, take care. Really the only challenge is to decide when to ask her out on a date, and that depends on where you are at on frame. You may be highly masculine, but just suck with women. In that case, you can ask her out after a week of limiting contact. Or you may be a soy boy simp. In that case, give it at least a month, and likely longer.

2. Hard Case. Here a lot of contact happens via phone. The problem here is that it is much easier to slip up and fall into her frame. Don't do that. Don't be tempted. Cut it off until you are ready. Stick with the rules: NEVER initiate contact, and Keep all contact she initiates short.

3. Harder Case: Physical meet ups, cool guy friends also present. As an example, suppose this is a great girl from Church and you all meet up after Mass for coffee in the Church Hall. There's a couple of cool guys, and a couple of girls, and her. In that case, your goal is to not be a gay friend. Instead talk to the guys and steer the conversation to manly interests. When the girls butt in and try to get you to emote, respond with awkward silence. Let it die, and then talk to the men again. Note she may try a shit test on you: a shaming tactic in front of her girl friends. There are various ways to reply, but let's keep it simple and go with amused mastery:

F: "Oh there he is. I thought you had left the country or something. I haven't heard from you."

M: Amused smirk. "Did I miss one of your texts?". You are amused because she fell into the trap. You DID reply, and you were pleasant (though brief). What she really is complaining about is that you have not been INITIATING texts and you haven't been chatting away like a faggot, which she is not used to, but she'll never admit to it.

F: "Well no, it's just that you haven't been around much to talk to."

M: "Yeah, I've been busy on this new Catholic Men's program. It takes up a lot of my time."

Then start talking fishing with the men.

If you are good, you could go with comedy:

F: "Oh there he is. I thought you had left the country or something. I haven't heard from you."

M: "You know, it's not healthy for you to obsess about me."

F: Stunned silence.

M: "I'm just messing with you. I've started on this Catholic Men's program and it's taking up all of my time."

Then talk fishing.

4. Hardest: Real life contact, simp guys. ALL that the men do is emote and talk about female crap. In this case, you just have to stop going. Now they are Catholic men, and they are your friends, so don't leave it there. Get them to start doing some manly activities with you, like camping. After a few outings, assume that you are back to the "Harder" case, and proceed.

Now you have something to talk about with the men, so you can start going back to the coffee.

5. Coming Clean: Suppose you ask her out on a date and she tells you she never thought of you in that way. At that point it's time to hit her with the truth. You aren't hiding anything, go back and read the mindset section – that is now your life. So you aren't being sneaky and there's nothing to be ashamed about. Hit her with the truth:

"Fair enough, but that is not how I view things. You're a great girl and I'd love to date you, but if that's not going to happen, that's just the way it is. I screwed this up, so I don't have any ill will towards you. Like I said, you are a great girl and I wish you the best.".

Note that this is a perfect time for her to try a good cry. Be ready for it and stand firm. Keep telling her, "Look, this was my fault. I think you are great, so don't worry about it."

She might try, "I don't want to lose you.". This is a test to get you to simp. Don't. "I told you the way I see things. I'm not interested in you as a friend, so continuing this is just going to be awkward.".

Note you will have to follow through and walk. She'll test you a few times, but keep up with the program of pleasant but short interaction. She may eventually hint at wanting to date.

6. The Final No: Lad, go back and review what I called this section. I am not promising that you will get this girl, just that you will escape the Friend Zone. You might have so screwed things up, that a date will never happen. Go in assuming a 50/50 chance. It's worth a try, but things are stacked against you. Even if you don't get this girl, you'll be a lot less

frustrated and a lot better off. This will strengthen your Frame no matter what the outcome, so it's worth it.

Alright, in either case, whether through game or escaping the friend zone, you are now dating. During the week after the date it is important, as before, that you do not initiate contact, except to call one time to set the particulars of the next date. Most likely she'll reach out to you and you handle it with the usual rules: pleasant, great hearing from her, had a great time, and keep it short. Of course if she reaches out to you then you can use that as an opportunity to set the next date. I'd say if it is the day after, tell her you'll give her a call later with the details.

At this point I'll list some key concepts that allow you to maintain Frame and grow her attraction:

1. NEVER have a fear of losing her. Don't be needy. Have an abundance mentality and always remember that you have tons of other women to pick from. Trust me, you are in the top 5% at this point in your life.

2. Do not blow up her phone and don't contact her via Social Media. Allow her to initiate contact except the one time you call with date details. Remember that you are the buyer, not the seller. Don't seek her approval.

3. The preference for communications between dates is voice communications over the phone. If she texts, text back to her to give you a call. The key when you are first starting out is to keep it short, but always be pleasant. "Hey, it's great to hear from you!" Short exchange and then "I have to run, but it's been great talking to you." Video calls are probably ok, but only if she initiates it, and remember to keep it short. After that comes texting, and finally social media. I'd avoid social media

all together if possible. And in case you missed it, let me repeat: KEEP IT SHORT.

4. Always remember that she is either a romantic interest or no interest.

5. If there is any flaking, avoid being butt hurt. Let her go and don't pursue. Tell her when she gets it figured out, to give you a call.

6. On flaking remember the two date rule. You ask her out twice. If the answer is not a definite yes, you still take her calls, but you stop asking. You also keep it short, because now she is no interest. As always, keep it pleasant.

7. Conversation should be natural, which for someone like you with Solid Frame, is the same thing as being authentic. Never brag. Never prove yourself. Never "win her over". You are the buyer, remember?

8. The overriding theme is that you are allowing her to experience your frame. You never enter into her frame.

9. Take advantage of opportunities to lead. Make decisions.

10. Avoid the temptation to prove to her you are a provider. If you followed the advice in this book, you have that covered. She'll get around to finding out about it, but let her ask, don't volunteer the information. Tell her about your job after she asks, and then drop it.

11. Always remember that women seek the validation of men. Therefore compliments are important. However, do not shower her with needless compliments. A woman does not feel validated from men she considers simps. If you pick up your

woman for a date, and she has spent time getting ready and looking nice for you, tell her she looks pretty.

The second date is the same as the first. A relaxed time that is a lot of fun. During this phase of dating you are evaluating her. The important thing you are checking out is the personality match. She's pretty. She does a great job walking around in those 5" heels. You love how she dresses. But she's a wallflower and talking to her is like pulling teeth. It's not working, and this means you have to end it.

For personality match, opposites attract. Maybe you are pretty extroverted and a wallflower works for you. That's fine. Generally a good pick for a girl is a mild to moderate extrovert. That's what I've gone for. However you just have to go by what works out. And if the personality doesn't match, you're going to have to end it.

Another thing you want to see is her feminine nature. A great way to evaluate this is to watch a chick flick with her. The go-to chick flick is the (2002) "Count of Monte Cristo". Yes that is a chick flick. The chick flick climax for the movie is when he yells out, "Do not rob me of my hate!". Observe your date during this scene. She should be glued to the screen and grin a bit. Of course the woman in the film, who your date is heavily identifying with, is going to rob the star of his hate. That's why your girlfriend is grinning, because she knows the woman is important to the star and that he will give up the hate for her.

A quick aside on female nature. Women will put themselves into a movie scene so that they can experience the emotion. Look, there's usually an embarrassing moment in a chick flick. Don't be surprised if your girlfriend is hiding behind a pillow during this scene and peaking over the top to watch. She's in the scene and she is actually embarrassed. This phenomenon is why women talk about problems instead of trying to fix them.

Listen to a conversation between women sometime: "Oh, you must have felt so embarrassed! I can imagine how you felt! Etc… etc… Women are emotional creatures. That is feminine, and that is what you want.

You now reach the point of regular dating. Here you want to take the lead and determine what the date will be. There are a lot of possibilities:

1. Swing Dancing. Always a winner.
2. Food dates of various types: coffee, dinner date, or brunch after Church.
3. Get togethers and parties.
4. Have a cook out. Grill or smoke some meat, and invite people over.
5. Picnics.
6. Walks.
7. Netflix night. Make sure to have some popcorn.
8. The surprise date. Remember to tell her how to dress. A good surprise date is the picnic.
9. Hiking.
10. Biking.
11. Boating if you have access to a boat. Pulling around one of those inflatable rings and letting her ride on it is always fun. Go easy on her, and make sure you have a minimum of 3 people on the boat, one to watch the rider at all times. Make sure the rider has a life vest on.
11. The grand daddy. A motorcycle ride to an eating establishment. Think bistro.

That's enough to get you started. You can repeat dates, just space it out.

So at this point you've been dating and now there are a few particulars you will want to know. I'll list them:

1. When should you hold hands? This is up to her. Let her do it. If she is especially shy, I'd say take her hand when you go on a walk through-the-park type date. Usually after 3 dates.

2. What about the three magic words: I Love You? Again, she should be the first one with that. Also, if you don't love her, don't respond in kind. You might still be evaluating, so be truthful about that. You might tell her, "You are a great girl, and I'm growing closer to you, but I'm not there yet." Expect your first fight after that, but keep it honest.

3. What about exclusive dating? That one again is up to her, because you'll be dating other women until then.

That last point brings up the pitfalls you should avoid. Let's go over them:

1. One-itis. Putting her on a pedestal (me Lady). She's the only one for you. You were meant for each other. It was ordained. You prayed, so this is the work of the Holy Ghost (unless you are a prophet and saw a huge light and heard a voice announce it, you have no idea if this is the one for you. Drop the B.S. and likely the Sin of Presumption.).

You are working on the most critical decision of your life, so you must take your time. You have no idea if she's "the one", that's why you are dating – to find out. One-itis also makes you look needy, which often times will drive her away.

2. Getting butt hurt over flaking or outright rejection. Look, she might like blond haired guys, and you have brown hair. She has concluded that you are not her type, just like you concluded the girl you found ugly wasn't your type, so you avoided approaching. If she rejects you, she is doing you a favor – you know where you stand. Getting butt hurt is weak and needy. It serves no purpose. Tell her it's fine, but you are

only interested in her romantically, and if she changes her mind to give you a call. Then stick by that, let her initiate contact, but otherwise move on. Don't ever whine, and don't ever blow up her phone with your whining and simping. Come on, do I even need to explain this?

3. Entering her frame. You are the man, you lead. Don't ever get emotional around her or start talking like a fag or a woman. Maintain Frame.

4. Failing a shit test. I think the best way to explain it is to give you an actual example of one which occurred during a phone conversation:

> Female: I ran into an old friend the other day, and my friend was telling me about work, (note the awkward avoidance of the male pronoun, yeah, obviously this was a guy), and my friend wants to visit, so HE wants to go out for breakfast on Saturday.
>
> Man: (Matter-of-fact tone) No, you are not going out on a date with some guy. Furthermore you are disrespecting me, and I don't want to talk to you. When you are ready to apologize, give me a call. Click. (A quick note, this was said calmly and did not come across as butt hurt. If anything, he was a little irate, but actually was laughing inside because this was so obvious).
>
> Female: (5 minutes later). Phone rings and she is on the other end crying and apologizing.
>
> Man: That's fine, but we agreed that we would only date each other, so don't let it happen again.

The man would fail the test if he had responded emotionally. Whining how they agreed to date exclusively; however never ordering her NOT to do it, instead using words like "should" and "would".

Another test is if a pretty girl walks by, and you check her out.

> Female: (irate) And what are you looking at?!

> Man: I was checking out that hot girl. I can't help myself, I'm attracted to beautiful women, which is why I'm dating you.

And finally the last example, a shit test that you absolutely can not ignore: Her texting while on a date. Nip that in the bud immediately:

> "I did not bring you on this date to sit here and watch you text. You either put that phone away or this date is over."

The shit test is her way to evaluate your Emotional Side of Frame. To pass, the main rule is not to whine or get emotional (in which case you fail). She's trying to see what kind of lifeguard you'll be. There are a variety of responses. You can Acknowledge and Ignore; for example if while driving to a restaurant she tells you she changed her mind and wants to go someplace else, you would tell her that's fine, but you are going to the restaurant you picked.

Another standby is the Agree and Amplify. You could have used it in the hot girl example I gave above. "I was looking at that hot chick (agreeing with what she is implying), there's so many to look at, you can get a stiff neck sometimes, but you are the only one for me.". The last part is called "comfort" in the manosphere. Sometimes she is just looking for some comfort, so a good way to do it without getting emotional is to tack it on to the end of an agree and amplify.

The default easy way out is to call her out on it, but have a smirk and roll with amused mastery. The key is to not whine. Basically you swat it away avoiding any emotional response to it.

Another way to pass a shit test that married men can use is to give your wife a spanking. "Look, if you don't knock it off, I'm throwing you over my lap and giving you a spanking." We'll go more into that later.

4. Sliding. You have it made, she's a great girl. So you allow laziness to cause you to lose frame. Maybe you stop working out. Maybe you get lazy and start repeating the same date over-and-over again. Maybe you let her take the lead and set the date because it is easier. You can't let your guard down, you have to Game for the rest of your life. Yes, the same lessons have application in marriage also.

5. Changing for her. Big mistake lads. She's attracted to you because of who you are. A lot of times "changing for her" means canceling activities with buddies so you can spend time with her. Now there is a balance, since a girl is an extra activity which requires time, so you will definitely see LESS of your buddies. However, never give up friends and hobbies. This means that at times <u>you have to tell her "No"</u> so you can go do something, e.g. hunting, with your friends. Let me stress this: if after some reflection you realize that you never tell her "No", you have a problem.

Those are some pitfalls to avoid. Learn them well.

Now I mentioned previously that you will be dating other women. The provider simps are having a heart attack. "What? This will upset me Lady! You should not do that! The Holy Ghost gave her to me, she's the one for me!"

Have you told each other that you love each other? Have you talked about being exclusive? Have you dated long enough to surface her flaws, and can you live with them? Seems like a lot can go wrong, so tell me again why you are only dating her. I'll tell you why, your frame is weaker than you thought. You think finding another quality girl like this one will be impossible for you. That is weak frame, so knock it off.

On a related note, if you are using an online dating app like Catholic Match, keep your profile up. When girls continue to reach out to you, chat them up and ask the promising prospects out on a date. If you aren't exclusive, keep dating other women.

Of course she will discover the other women, but that's fine. It will be a shit test. You can have some fun with it: "Forget about those other girls baby, that's just a thing. What you and I have is real.". Tell her "Gentlemen don't kiss and tell. Do you honestly believe those other girls are better than you? Come on." Note that her discovery of the hussies sniffing around her man might lead to the next phase where you date exclusively. If you think she's marriage material, then do it. This also means you have to be honorable and keep your word. No other women -- men keep their word. However you can continue with some Dread Game, which I discuss later.

Now as you get more serious, things change. She should be calling you a lot more. About once per week you also reach out to her an additional time and initiate contact. As always, you maintain frame throughout and lead, avoiding the pitfalls. Another rule that is relaxed is that you can now date more than once per week. Things have changed, so the rules get modified. But note, don't rush this and use it as an excuse to simp. Make sure you have done a thorough evaluation as this will take at least a month, and usually longer.

As things get more serious, she will want to know more about provision. That is to be expected and this is why when dating exclusively you start to add some provision. I want you to understand that there should be a natural shift. Normally she should bring it up, but if you bring it up as part of natural conversation, this is now acceptable. You have to be careful here, because this could be you resorting to simping and losing Frame. However if you are talking about you plans for the summer, say a summer internship, then it would be natural to also talk about future employers and plans.

Another part of provision is to start doing things for her. Look, provision is not evil, it's actually going to be your job duty as her husband. She's going to want to see that you have this ability. The key here is balance: demonstrate your ability, but out of real love for her. Don't do it to simp or prove yourself. Again the key is to trust your Frame. You have followed the program laid out earlier, so you have provision covered and don't need to prove anything. She'll discover it, you don't have to force it. But yes, at this stage it is perfectly fine to drive over to her house to change her flat. I'd make it somewhat transactional, though mention payment AFTER the fact. The tire has been plugged, you are a little dirty, and you look at her: "Where are the brownies? I drive over here to fix this flat, and there aren't any brownies?". As always, evaluate requests to see if they are shit tests (will they cause you to lose frame?) and sometimes say no. However as you get more serious you will add in more provision. Also, remember to keep your hobbies and friends. <u>If you are never saying "no" to her, that's a big red flag that you are simping.</u>

While dating your woman, it is also important to neg her and to mess with her in general, in a playful way. I've gone over how to escape a neg, and you should go back and review "Cockroach Game" as a good example, but here's a list of comments to escape the neg:

1. I was just messing with you.
2. Be real. (A meaningless phrase that will confuse her).
3. Quit trying so hard. (This is used during an approach where you are implying she is flirting with you instead of the other way around.)
4. You're being immature, you need to grow up. The tactic here is to piss her off so she forgets the neg. You'll spin up her hamster wheel and the bearings will be smoking. Women hate being called immature. After you feed emotion to her, then you say, "Didn't I tell you I was messing with you?".

Being playful with your girlfriend is important, so go ahead and mess with her a little.

So now you are in a serious exclusive relationship. The obvious next step is marriage. First I'm assuming that she is high quality, as I outlined above. She's cooked some meals for you, is feminine, and she's a good Catholic. You also want to make sure she's not saddled with $100,000 of student debt, because you my friend will be the one paying that bad boy off. But I'm assuming that you have all of that covered and she's definitely marriage material. When should you get married?

I'd say that at a bare minimum you have dated for two years. Longer is better. Also the optimum if you are in college is to get engaged your senior year after you have a job offer. If you interned your Junior year summer, chances are you have at least one offer. The wedding generally will then be in the Fall after you graduate and have already started working. Make sure your employer knows you'll need the time off for your wedding.

My general advice on marriage is to get married young. You'll hear a lot of people tell you to wait and live life for awhile. In my opinion this is bad advice for a good Catholic. First the good Catholic Trad girls (you know the ones, they cook your dinner while wearing an apron and heels) will be snapped up early leaving you with slim pickings. Also the people giving you this advice are sometimes heathens or even Prots who have a hole in their lives where God should be. Get married early and have kids while your wife is young and you both have energy.

The tradition on proposing is to ask her Dad's permission, and then propose. Proposing is done down on one knee. If your hands shake while doing it, don't get bummed out, that is a common occurrence. Now afterward comes the wedding planning. Your only responsibility is to plan the honeymoon, so do a detailed job with that. Everything else she will do, because you really could care less what pattern your dinner plates are. This is one of the few times in your life where the woman really leads. However, if you have maintained Frame throughout your dating relationship, she will come to you to make decisions. Here is a little trick to dodge that bullet:

Female: Honey, I can't decide what pattern to get for the plates. I like the Wittenburg Rose but the Hereford Blue is kind of pretty. Which one should we pick?

Man: (saying a quick thank you to the author of *The Catholic Red Pill* for warning about this) Yeah, those are good picks. <u>Which one do you like better</u>?

Female: I really like that Wittenburg Rose but the Hereford is pretty.

Man: I like the Wittenburg better. Go with that.

Trust me lads, this actually works. Now some men may argue that this was a shit test. I disagree. She is reflexively coming to you for a decision, and this is a very good sign that you have

Solid Frame. She's also getting some comfort because weddings stress out women.

As far as the wedding, it flies by. The only notable part is the vows. You really feel the presence of God during your vows because you are making a solemn vow before Him and He is sending you Grace. After that, make sure to give her compliments where due on her looks and her dress. The Wedding Day is the special day women think about all during their teenage years. She's the star of this show. My other advice is to try not to drink too much. This can be hard as you will be running in to old friends and relatives you haven't seen in awhile, so the temptation is to have a drink with each one of them. Avoid that if possible.

I want to also talk about "the next day". The next day you'll be doing some introspection to see if you feel any different. The answer is no, except it will hit you that you now have a HUGE responsibility. You now must protect and provide for this woman for the rest of your life, as well as any kids that come along. Getting hit with the gravity of this situation is perfectly normal; most men go through it. Don't worry about it, you have Solid Frame and you can handle it. Now over time the Grace of marriage grows and before long you will actually start to feel the connection you have with your wife. But that takes time. And this brings us to the next section.

Married Life

Either you were married when you bought this book, or you plan on eventually getting married, which should be attainable if you follow the program I laid out. The first thing I want to discuss is a controversy in some circles over Natural Family Planning (NFP). I guess I also need to point out in this day-and-age that artificial contraception is a mortal sin, which includes the use of condoms, IUDs, and birth control pills. That's not allowable and you'll burn in hell if you do it anyhow.

Now getting back to NFP, there is a lot of bad advice out there. In general, NFP is allowable -- there is only the requirement for serious reasons. If you are a new couple starting out and are saving for a house (because you want to have kids), that is a serious reason. If you have a toddler who is not potty trained yet, you have a serious reason. If the husband is going to some graduate school, you have a serious reason. If the wife is homeschooling, you have a serious reason. If you want to save money to buy a high end car, you DON'T have a serious reason. One thing to note, there is ZERO requirement to ask permission from a priest. That is a common error.

For those of you with scruples, I want to present to you the teaching of the Catholic Church long before Vatican II. You can find this on the CMRI website, which is an order of hard core sede-Traditional Catholics (they believe we have not had a Pope since Pope Pius XII). This is not a leftist liberal group:

> The very concept of "rhythm" was first considered by the Catholic Church in 1853. The Bishop of Amiens, France, submitted the following question to the Sacred Penitentiary:
>
> "Certain married couples, relying on the opinion of learned physicians, are convinced that there are several days each month in which conception cannot occur. Are those who do

not use the marriage right except on such days to be disturbed, especially if they have legitimate reasons for abstaining from the conjugal act?"

On March 2, 1853, the Sacred Penitentiary (during the reign of Pope Pius IX) answered as follows:

"Those spoken of in the request <u>are not to be disturbed</u>, providing that they do nothing to impede conception."
a) Please note: "providing that they do nothing to impede conception." When married couples practice rhythm, they do not do anything unnatural in the act itself.

In Medical Ethics by Fr. Charles J. McFadden, O.S.A, Ph.D., we read:

"In the use of the safe period, married persons do not interfere in any way with the operation of nature. Their marital relationship is carried out in the strictly natural manner... No unnatural action is committed by those who exercise their marital rights in a truly natural manner during the safe period... In marriage, both parties acquire mutual permanent rights to marital relationship. This fact indicates that they have the right at all times. Generally speaking, however, they do not have the obligation to exercise their rights at any specific time."

Those are the facts. The Church teaches that you can use NFP for serious reasons. Look, if you are good Catholics and end up with 4 kids, you've done your part. Follow the Church's teaching and you'll be fine.

Now in married life the man is in charge, and the wife is to submit to his leadership. He has final authority. The only exception is if he orders her to commit a sin, in which case she is obligated to refuse. You've seen the bible verses: 1 Peter 3,

Colossians 3, Ephesians 5, and 1 Tim 2. So how do you put this in practice?

You could look at this like a master/slave relationship. He barks orders and she obeys. That fails the gut check test, and it also does not seem to comport with the admonition for husbands to love their wives. So again, how do you put this in practice?

The manosphere has developed a most excellent model that will help you in sorting this out. They call it the Captain and First Officer. Now on a ship the Captain has ultimate authority; he has to be obeyed. Directly under him is his First Officer, also called the Executive Officer or XO. He (in this case she) is his second in command and has his own authority which derives from the captain's. A good captain routinely talks things over with his XO, and he gives his XO authority to carry out his duties in his own sphere. Now if the captain believes that the XO has made a mistake, he will step in and countermand the XO's order, but day-to-day he lets the XO carry out his duties and there is an overriding relationship of mutual respect (but NOT mutual submission like some heretics have wrongly stated).

This is a great model for married life. You are the Captain, and your wife is your XO. When important decisions are to be made, you will collaborate with your wife and seek input, but you will make the final decision. In other areas, you won't even be involved in her decisions, but you always have the right to step in if you deem it necessary. On her part she needs to look after matters pertaining to her sphere, e.g. run the household and raise the kids, but she also is obliged to obey and support decisions made by her husband. Here is your answer lads.

Now as far as living the married life, the first thing to understand is the serious responsibility placed on you to provide, and to protect your wife and kids. Just as important is your responsibility to lead. This is critical when it comes to living a Catholic life. If you have followed the program in this book, you will have a good paying job. However when work is over and you come home, your second job starts up again. You have to lead, play an important part in your family's lives, and make sure that they are good Catholics. This is a huge responsibility, so how do you pull it off?

As always in these circumstances, there is usually a virtuous mean, with errors of deficit and errors of excess on either side. Let's go over the problems first, and then I'll give you some guidance on how to maintain a virtuous mean.

First is the error of deficit. You come home, sit down and watch Netflix war documentaries all night, taking a break for dinner. On the weekend you go golfing, and maybe after Mass on Sunday you take the family out for a meal. If you can go through your married life without ever falling into this rut, you are a better man than me (or you had the benefit of a great book to read). This behavior is understandable: you come home brain dead after a commute, and you are worn out. You just want to chill. And so you do.

Next is the error of excess. There are cases of men coming home from work and cooking the dinner. He also does a lot of the house chores (remember, she doesn't work) and it is obvious to everyone she is a lazy slob. I have advice for this situation: never apologize for working. This means you accept that working takes a lot out of you and that she has responsibilities herself as the stay-at-home Mom. Keep in mind that homemakers also have more flexibility than you and can take breaks. Don't apologize for working.

So where is the mean? On one hand you will definitely be brain dead from work. On the other hand she also needs a break and some alone time. So how do you balance this out? In my opinion you accept that you will be worn out when you come home. So you do take some leisure time. The best way to do this is to set dinner time about 45 minutes to an hour after you come home. During that time you change and then relax. Perhaps you fire up the internet and check the news and read a few articles. Whatever is relaxing. The nice part is that you use dinner time as the alarm clock that announces that leisure time is over. You have a relaxing dinner with the family, and then you take the kids and tell your wife to go relax. You have it. You play with the kids, and then work with your wife to get them to bed on time. After that you can hit the weight pile and finish up the night.

That's my suggestion. You might have another plan to accomplish this balance. The important part is to find the virtuous mean. Accept your need for some leisure, but don't get sucked in and spend all of your time on your leisure activities. Be part of your family and give your wife a little break at the same time.

Another important responsibility is to take charge and plan family activities. Again, being worn out from work and not having a good plan for some responsible leisure time will get in the way of this. If you don't have kids yet, remember to plan a date night every weekend, or mix it up and plan a daytime event like a picnic or a hike. This is a good opportunity to lead. When the kids come, plan things to do with the whole family. Don't over complicate things. Going to the park to look for pine cones is a fun outing.

General Advice for Marriage

1. Be playful. Here's an actual exchange. I was working on the computer when the wife came into my office. I stopped what I was doing and swung my chair around:

> Wife: The light is burned out in the laundry room. (Note she was quite pleased with herself as she got to hint.)
>
> Me: Man….. that's tough. It must be so hard on you to do laundry without the light. That's so hard. So hard. I feel for you.
>
> Wife: (confused look. I actually triggered the "girl talk" part of her brain.) But the light is burned out.
>
> Me: I know… I know, that's so hard. Share. Share. I'm here for you.
>
> Wife: (figured out I was messing with her. Hands on hips). ARE YOU GOING TO CHANGE THE LIGHT BULB?
>
> Me: Why do you have to always do this? We were having a moment, and you are always trying to fix things!
>
> Wife. At this point she had had enough of the fun and launched. There was pinching and tickling and rolling around on the floor. I eventually went and changed the light bulb for her.

Another playful time. This happened a few times, so this is a "typical" time. Imagine you were a guest at my house for Thanksgiving. I'm in the kitchen helping my wife with the turkey. While pulling the turkey out of the oven I spot a convenient spatula sitting on the counter. This is what you would have heard:

Wife: "No! Don't you do it! Bad, you are so bad." (Pop).

At that point you see my wife come tearing out of the kitchen and I'm chasing her getting in a few good "pats" on her bottom with the spatula. At some point she got tired of the game and wheeled around. Again pinching, tickling, and rolling around on the floor ensued. I eventually got her across my lap and gave her a few more "pats", then leaped up and did an NFL touchdown victory strut. Then we went back to the kitchen and I went to work slicing up the turkey.

One final example I'll call the "push off". This sounds a bit ludicrous, and I'll admit this doesn't make sense since it is obviously fake, but all I can say is try this out sometime. Here's how it would go down. I'd grab my wife and start kissing her. Then I'd abruptly stop and push her off perhaps a foot, and start saying, "No… No, you're just not into it. This just isn't….", at which point her eyes would be popping out of her head. Then I'd grab her again and kiss her some more, then push her off again, and say the same kind of stuff. She'd end up saying something like, "You're such a mess." Why did it work? All I can do is answer with a question, "Why do women love watching chick flicks?".

So I hope that gives you a general idea. Be playful with your wife. Chase her around. Get into a pillow fight. Have fun.

2. Dread Game. First what it isn't. You are at a party with your girlfriend and she is being bitchy. You respond by going to another girl and talking to her to make your girlfriend jealous. This is NOT Dread Game. While it may actually work short term, this is weak behavior and will end up disgusting your girlfriend.

Dread Game starts with the girl's ultimate fantasy: sticking her tongue out at other women who are lusting after her man. Dread Game is used on your girlfriend and your wife. It is ultimately a compliment to her, which you will understand shortly.

To start, you must get into the habit of natural light flirting with other women. Here we go back to the handy retail clerk. You should use opportunities that present themselves to lightly flirt, even throwing in some negs until it becomes something you automatically do. When you reach this level Dread Game will be something you do without even thinking about it.

Here's a situation where you use Dread Game. You are out with your wife at a high end restaurant having a romantic dinner. A hot waitress comes up to the table to take your order and you naturally flirt with her and throw in a neg. Now remember that women have ten times the social awareness of men, so the waitress will pick up on this and flirt back. But there's another woman in the scene who has high social awareness – your wife. Right now the provider simps are losing their mind. But...But, me lady will be displeased with me. This is so dishonorable!

Wrong. Your wife will get a bit angry (feeding her emotions lad), but not with you. Never with you. She'll be pissed off by the other woman sniffing around her man. She'll most likely make physical contact with you, perhaps touching your hand. And guess what, in the end she "wins" against the other woman, proverbially sticking her tongue out at her, which is a very high compliment for her that will pay off later.

Other elements of Dread Game include going out with your buddies without explaining yourself to "me Lady", and if you are single, leaving your profile up on a Catholic Dating Site while you are in a casual relationship with a woman. I think after you are in an exclusive relationship you have to take down your profile however.

A quick aside, men have a weakness that women instinctively know about, and that is physical touch. There is a particular part they aim for and that is the upper arm / tricep area. Observe sometime if your wife or girlfriend wants you to do something and see if she tries to touch you there. Unfortunately it's a pretty brutal move and we don't have a lot of defense against it.

Women also have a weak spot, and that is their elbows. Come up behind your wife or girlfriend, and without startling her, "hug" her from behind and grab her opposite elbow with each hand. So your right hand is holding her left elbow and vice versa. She will melt. And so ends the aside.

3. Spanking. No, you are not going to spank your wife as an act of punishing her. This is part of being playful, though the symbolism is good (up with the patriarchy!). I also have discovered that giving your wife a spanking solves two problems. First, there are times when you find yourself in a petty argument that is getting destructive. You pull rank and tell her that the argument is over, but she won't stop. At that point you say, "Look, this argument is over. If you keep at it, I'm giving you a spanking.". This will guarantee that she will keep at it, so you end up chasing her around the house (the argument has now been turned into something playful), and you'll end up on the floor with her claws flying until you can get her over your lap.

The other thing the spanking solves is a shit test. There are times when she throws an obvious shit test at you and you're not in the mood to play that game. So you say, "Knock it off, or you're getting a spanking.". The outcome is the same, she'll keep going because she wants the spanking, so you'll end up chasing her around the house again.

On the playful side, every once in awhile you need to grab your wife and start wrestling with her. Maybe start it off with a pillow fight (one word of caution, LIGHTLY tap her with the pillow, women really aren't as used to the horseplay as men are), and you all end up rolling around the floor with her tickling and pinching, and you maneuvering her over your lap.

4. "I don't deserve you". Let's shift gears and talk about something you should avoid at all costs. I don't know how many times I've been disgusted to hear men say a variant of this in front of other people: "I don't deserve you.". "I don't know how I lucked out and got someone as great as my wife.". "Happy wife, happy life.". "She's the boss.". What's worse, they say this crap in front of her FEMALE friends. You should see the look on the woman's face when her husband pulls this stunt. Do you remember the woman's ultimate fantasy? You are doing the exact freaking opposite. This is extremely insulting to your wife: you are a loser, and that's all she could get; a fact that you are broadcasting to her girlfriends. Don't ever do this. You are way better off being arrogant (don't do this) and saying in front of her friends how lucky SHE is to have you. That still sucks, but trust me, it would be better.

5. Date night. One of your jobs is to plan the weekly date night with just your wife. This becomes critical after your first born kid is a year old or maybe a bit younger. Because before then you won't be having date night as you both will be exhausted and its tough leaving a tiny baby with your parents. But the time will come when you realize you both are ready for dating again.

Now your wife will be scared to death. She'll have horrible fantasies of savage moslems sneaking into your house and stealing the baby. Be ready for it and ignore her. Plan everything: get the babysitting lined up, parents or in-laws are the best, and make reservations. For the first outing plan on something that won't take too long like a bistro type dinner date. She'll love it, and then you can get back to full date mode, maybe even a "romantic weekend getaway" at some point.

6. Friends and Hobbies. As I've written before, it is important not to change for her. Maintain your guy friends and keep doing your hobbies. Of course you have to find the virtuous mean when it comes to balancing family time with hobby time, however it is important for you to continue with your hobbies. Also note that as your sons get older it is a good practice to bring the boys along when you go out with the men.

7. Lead. Take care of your budget. Set up family outings and date nights. Make decisions. You are the captain, you are the lifeguard, and that is what your wife wants and expects.

8. Family prayer. Your number one job is to get your wife and children into heaven, so you also must lead in family prayer. Say the Grace before Meals. Also gather in the evening and lead your wife and any kids in prayer. Note please avoid the hour long pious torture session. Remember your State in Life, you are not an abbot leading a monastery. 15 minutes is about right.

Problems in Marriage

Instead of starting with some rules to follow, I'm going to go over various cases that might apply to you, and give you a road map of how to fix the problem. In general the solution is the same: maintain Solid Frame.

1. The Drunk Captain. This is the most common problem, but fortunately the easiest to fix. You are a masculine man with a good job. You don't take crap from your wife. You'll allow a little nagging, but put her in her place from time-to-time….. and you abuse this. You do your own thing, and you've been this way for awhile. Your wife is cold, she nags, and the bedroom is not great. You know you are messing up, but how do you fix this?

First, you have to deal with the root cause, and I've already gone over this. Follow my advice on establishing RESPONSIBLE leisure time after work. You are worn out after work, so up to an hour of leisure will be beneficial to your marriage, but you have to cut it off. This is probably how you ended up as the drunk captain, getting burned out, and then swinging hard the other way and just doing your own thing. There is a reasonable middle ground, and you have to get back to that.

Second, in the case of the drunk captain there is invariably an addiction. It might be watching TV. It might be browsing the internet, watching Youtube or Netflix. Or it might be computer games or console games. If it's not an addiction, then it is going out with your buddies too much, almost exclusively. If it's addiction, follow the advice on addiction breaking I wrote about previously. If you are golfing too much, find a responsible balance.

Third, you aren't leading (again, because you are worn out). This is why your wife is nagging you. She wants you to captain the ship, so do it. This oftentimes shows up as letting chores slip and not going out on dates.

Finally, you probably need to work on your Frame, and with the Drunk Captain, this usually is the physical side of frame. You quit working out, or you got fat, or your clothes look like crap, or maybe your hair looks bad. You know what to do.

The good thing about the Drunk Captain is that it is easy to fix and your wife will pick up on the change and change her own behavior. Oftentimes you can get this completely fixed in a month, so start today.

2. The Hard Case. You are married to a stay-at-home Catholic wife and you provide for your family. You yourself are a good Catholic. However you aren't very masculine and you are a push over, the proverbial provider simp. Your wife sometimes bosses you around, and you don't have a lot of energy. When she's not nagging, maybe she's ignoring you. Maybe you waste time on addictions, or maybe you are busy obeying your nagging wife. The bedroom sucks. This is the case of good provision with low attraction. What to do?

This is all around weak frame. To start, cheer up a bit. You've been reading this book and you know it has the answers, so you are already fixing things just by finding out what to do. That's a good thing. Second, give yourself time. I'd say you won't see huge improvements for a good six months, but you'll see improvements within a month, which will keep you going.

So you know you have weak frame, and you already know the obvious answer – you have to go through the program and develop solid frame. The best place to start is the physical side of frame, basically because you see results pretty fast and that will motivate you. In your case you need a lot of work on the emotional side, as well as hitting the Spiritual and Intellectual, but we'll get to that.

You've read the detailed program, but in short, if you are pudgy, switch to Atkins and cut the weight. Don't bother about the clothes or the haircut until you get in shape. This means you also have to hit the weight pile, maybe starting with some pushups. After your body is in shape, then up the wardrobe and consider a new hair cut.

Concurrently if possible, start on the emotional side. Certainly read the books I listed. Now going up to the Bakken for the summer to work on an all-male work crew is not possible, so you have to do something different (in addition to the other things to work on in the program). For this I recommend doing some all-male activities. Develop some hobbies that you can do with your male friends. Go hunting or fishing once a month with the men. If you don't know how, lose the pride and ask them to teach you. Or maybe work out with a buddy. Upping hobbies and having some all-male activities will give your emotional side a needed boost.

Finally, ignore negative behavior from your wife, even in the bedroom. You have to own your life. You are the man, you are in charge, you have the responsibility. She's going to be negative for a little while because you haven't been doing your job. Own it, then fix it. Don't get butt hurt, and never whine again if you've been doing that.

If you are patient, put in the work, and give it six months, you'll be amazed at how much better your life will be. And it could be worse.

3. The Harder Case. You and your wife both work, and maybe she makes more money than you. Because of this you have to

warehouse your kids in strangercare. The only thing in your favor is that you and your wife are both Catholics. Beyond that, when she is not nagging you, she is disrespectful and even makes fun of you from time to time. You feel like a loser, because you are a loser. Your bedroom is dead. This is the case of low provision and NO attraction. What to do?

Again, cheer up a little; you have the book, you have the answers, so you can fix this. However since provision is low, this is going to take a long time, and furthermore due to low provision it might be awhile until your wife respects you. IF you can get a better job in short order, you can get this repaired in a year, but you have to steel yourself, this might take 4 years to fix. I'm sorry, but that's reality. You are a man, and you will deal with it.

Where will you be when you get this fixed? Your wife is going to quit her job and she's going to raise the kids. You'll have a job that allows you to support your family. On top of that you will be physically fit and start living a rewarding life. Some night you'll slap your wife on the ass and that will lead to a fun night in the bedroom. I'd say that's a lot of benefit, so get fired up and get started.

To begin, develop Solid Frame. Go through the program, and do what I've already outlined in the Hard case. However since your provision is low, don't expect things to get a whole lot better with your wife. Now you should expect some improvement, but every morning when she is forced to kennel the kids, she's going to resent you. That's natural. Own it and fix it.

On provision, you are facing some constraints. It is highly unlikely that you can take time off from your job as the Walmart greeter to retool. In this case you will have to find a program that allows you to get an online degree or online certifications. This means you are going to have to do a lot of homework checking out which professions pay well and are attainable. A good place to start is Governor's Western University, which is an accredited university program that is completely online. You can also look into the I.T. world where Certifications are very important and can land you a good paying job. Give yourself a full two months to research this. Again, that's just for research. Put the effort in. Query the government database on starting salaries and median income for the profession. Check out the online programs. Get advice from other men. Network. You have to get the provision problem solved, so put as much work into fixing this as you do in developing frame.

One final note, there is a site called the married red pill: https://www.reddit.com/r/marriedredpill/ I don't know much about Reddit, but I've read some of their material. A lot of the advice is good, some of it is immoral, but it will help you out. Create an anonymous Reddit account and start hanging out there. The guys who run that Reddit provide a free service called, "Own Your Shit Weekly" where you start by doing a full dump of your problems and go over your improvement plan. Then you check in weekly and report progress and where you screwed up. The men can be brutal, but you are anonymous and it is likely you need to hear it. Give this a try as you have a long row to hoe and will need support.

I want to put out a challenge to the other men reading this book. I think we need a Catholic version of "married red pill". I'm counting on some of you to step up and set up a sub reddit to host this. Get together on the Suscipe Domine forum and plan it out. Another alternative is to use VOAT, which protects you from being blocked. I'll support it and even be one of the moderators, but I want others to take the lead on this.

But remember, it could be worse:

4. The Impossible Case. I hate the word impossible, but I had to cook this up because there is probably going to be one like this. However, even if this describes you, don't give up immediately, especially if you have kids. Pray for her conversion. What am I talking about?

She's not Catholic and she won't have sex without contraception. This means Mortal Sin, and you are toast. On top of that you basically fit the description of the Hardest Case. This may be an impossible case. What to do?

First, quit sinning. You aren't going to get anywhere being an enemy of the Lord. He still loves you and wants to save you, but you have to repent and turn back to God. Give up the contraception and take your lumps. Actually if you have a dead bedroom, maybe it will buy you time to fix this.

Second, get Spiritual advice as soon as possible from a solid Traditional priest. Find out what your options are. This may end in a legal divorce / separation, or a legal divorce / annulment. You need guidance from a good priest.

Third, consult with a divorce attorney as a protective measure. If she files for divorce against you, you want to be prepared. Kids need a father, and taking preparatory measures will give you a better chance of being part of their lives.

Finally, get working on Frame. Go over The Hard Case and The Hardest Case and start putting in the work. If you can delay a confrontation over the contraception, that's a good thing. It will give you time to work on your frame. If this works out, after you have Solid Frame you can have a long talk with your wife. However you will be in a much better position where she respects you and is even attracted to you. Perhaps you can talk her into using NFP and eventually to convert to the Faith.

But of course this could end badly, while you are still weak. She can ask for sex and you'll say no, not with contraception. You'll tell her you are living a Catholic life now, and guaranteed this will set her off. There will be constant fighting and eventually she'll file for divorce. Remember the old adage, prepare for the worst, and hope for the best.

These cases go over some typical problems in marriage – from the easily fixed to the impossible. In every case a big part of the solution is to restore Solid Frame. At this point in the book, that should not come as a surprise.

Sex

If some of the younger lads skipped the first part of the book to get to the part on Game, still others went right for this section. I'm sorry to disappoint you, but there will be nothing graphic discussed. However there are some important concepts that married men need to know about.

Types of Sex. The most important thing to learn is to realize that there are four types of sex, which I'll go over with you. After you learn this, chances are any confusion you have been having will be resolved. Also note that this is not scientific, these are just 4 buckets I've created to help orientate you to the concepts:

1. Fun Sex. Fun sex does not usually involve a lot of planning. This is sex that you and your wife will look back on and joke about on your 20th wedding anniversary. The classic examples include the newly weds. They may sneak over to the neighbors back yard in the middle of the night to have sex – because they are newly weds. Or they might sneak out onto their roof in the middle of the night to have sex.

Another example is the "Mile High Club", which means having sex on an airplane, usually an international flight. Closely related is the "Sneak Your Newly Wed Wife into an Oil Refinery and Have Sex 100 ft. up on top of the Fluid Catalytic Cracking Unit Club" (the FCCU usually has a convenient industrial elevator). Their annual convention is usually a lot of fun.

Then there is the basic unplanned opportunities. You take your wife out on a picnic, look around and realize that you and her are the only people within a five mile radius. So things progress as you would expect.

The key takeaway for Fun Sex is to take advantage of the opportunities if they present themselves, but don't worry about it. It is rare, but the fun involved and the memories it will create are worth it.

2. Lazy Sex. I don't need to describe this, the name tells you everything. Lazy Sex usually starts after the kids arrive. The choice is either Lazy Sex or no sex, so you go with Lazy Sex. It happens and will play at least some role in every couple's sex life, especially if they have kids.

The key takeaway with Lazy Sex is to try to minimize it. Being conscious of it is a great start. However don't beat yourself up too much if you have little kids running around and spend a lot of your time sleep deprived. It's going to happen.

3. Intimate Sex. This is the bedrock of your married sex life. Intimate Sex usually starts a few hours outside of the bedroom, perhaps you take her out on a romantic dinner. It involves deep conversation and heavy flirting. This then can progress into the jacuzzi tub, and then ends up in the bedroom. In the bedroom there can be back rubs, foot massages (a must), and there's a lot of deeply felt "I Love You's". Intimate Sex comes from the provision side of marriage – she feels protected and loved. Remember I told you provision is not evil, it's part of your job description. Ideally Intimate Sex takes up the majority of your sex life, though it depends on her personality. Intimate Sex ultimate communicates this message to her: "I value you".

4. Hot Sex. Hot Sex is aggressive and physical. There is no "I Love You" during Hot Sex. This is the opportunity for your wife to profess, "You are the man, and you have authority over me". Instead of giving your wife a back rub, you'll be grabbing her by the hair, slapping her butt, grabbing her by the wrists, talking dirty to her, and making her confess how naughty she is.

One trick I heard about which will help you understand this better is called the Closet Door Trick. You set up the bedroom by leaving the closet door slightly ajar. While in the bedroom you throw your wife up against the door. Because it is ajar it gives way avoiding any injury, however it makes a loud bang. This will heighten the experience for your wife.

Hot Sex usually starts outside of the bedroom in a very physical way. You grab your wife. You kiss her for an extended time, 5 seconds minimum. You whisper naughty things to her. You slap her on the bottom. This then leads to the bedroom, which she'll be looking forward to. You may even pick her up and carry her into the bedroom.

Hot Sex ultimately sends the message to your wife: "I Want You.". It comes from the Attractive Side of your relationship. Why is this important? Consider two cases. In the first case your wife's sex life exclusively involves Intimate Sex. After awhile she will be tempted to think you are an over sensitive sissy. In the second case there is a mix of Hot Sex and Intimate Sex. Will she think you are overly emotional during Intimate Sex when a few days ago you had her by the hair and were thrashing her around on the bed? Of course not, which leads to an important point: Hot Sex allows your wife to fully enjoy the pampering she'll get during Intimate Sex (plus she'll like the Hot Sex).

So that's it for my classification system. I hope this has opened your eyes. Next, let's talk about the ideal proportions for each type. A typical scenario might be less than 1% Fun Sex, 10% Lazy Sex, 35% Hot Sex, and 55% Intimate Sex. Note that this is highly dependent on personality type, e.g. a Wallflower might want 80% Hot Sex. But this gives you a general ideal. Note I left Lazy Sex in as part of the ideal. We have to practice Prudence and not be utopians.

<u>The Dead Bed.</u> Maybe you are in a marriage where sex is very infrequent, and when it does happen it might be 90% Lazy Sex and 10% intimate sex. Your wife is bored and unenthused. You've just read my classifications and you are thinking, "Dang, I know what I have to do – introduce some Hot Sex, but how do I get there?". Here are the key points in fixing this situation, because it is not that simple:

1. Don't ever whine or get butt hurt. Your wife's behavior is reasonable and sane. Own your screw up and get it fixed. If your wife turns you down for sex, be pleasant, but leave her company and go back to reading one of the books I've listed that will help you strengthen your frame.

2. You've guessed it, you are probably suffering from weak frame. You know the score, run the program and develop Solid Frame.

3. Maybe you are very masculine, and in your personal and work life you own your shit, but around your wife you behave like a providing simp because that is what you thought you needed to do. For you, go back and read the sections on female nature and start treating her like a woman and lead her. In your case you can get this solved pretty quickly.

4. Especially for the men with weak frame, give yourself time. At best you will get this fixed at a minimum of 6 months out. If you have weak frame and zero game, it will be a year or longer. I'm sorry, but we are men, and we deal in facts. Run the program and get it fixed. Start with some pushups tonight.

5. A lack of hobbies, skills, and male friends oftentimes plays a part. You never say "No" to her, and "you changed for her". This needs to be fixed, so put into practice what I presented.

6. After you are far along in strengthening your Frame, you will need to start some Dread Game. As a review, the following is NOT Dread Game: "You're out on a date with your wife, and she announces that she won't be having sex tonight because she has a headache. So you start flirting with a girl." This is not Dread; this is disgusting, weak behavior. Instead, work on practicing light flirting at the reliable convenience store so that you will naturally flirt with some women in front of your wife.

Also, when you have reached the point in your program where you are upping your wardrobe after cutting down to 14% body fat and obtaining the V shape, THAT is part of Dread. She might say, "Wow, you've really started looking good, is this something I should be worried about?". You handle it as a shit test: "No, women definitely notice me, but I'm a good Catholic man." (Of course this might mean you have access to the confessional – let her worry about that).

7. Pay attention to what I said about being playful and giving your woman a spanking from time to time. Physical and Fun will oftentimes lead to sex.

8. Start being the Captain again and leading your wife. Plan activities and dates and handle your shit.

9. Hot Sex. Do NOT read this section, skip the months of work, and try to immediately have Hot Sex. You will freak her out. Instead, AFTER putting in the work and getting the results, start introducing it. A great way (and actually very likely to happen) is to do it when SHE initiates sex, which will happen if you have developed Solid Frame and have been running Dread on her. At that point, whisper in her ear, "You dirty little tramp, I can't believe you said that."; then it's off to the races.

In other cases, especially if your wife is shy, you will initiate it. The best way to introduce Hot Sex is after a work out. You've finished up with the weight pile, and come into the living room with your wife present. You immediately grab her and kiss her for a long time. Then you whisper in her ear, "you hot little wench" and slap her on the butt. Then gauge her response. 90% of the time she'll be turned on, and then it's off to the bedroom. 10% of the time she might be a little shocked. In that case you say, "Hey, I just got done with my manly workout and saw my hot little wife, what do you expect me to do?". Then do it again. She'll catch on.

After that, wring out the lazy sex, and get back to a good balance. But remember, you are in a hole starting out, so this will take some time.

Parenting Skills

I debated whether to put this section in the book. My motivation for writing this book is two fold:

1. Looking around and seeing the weak, simping men, especially the younger generation. Men who have been brain washed and are living miserable lives. Men don't leave their brothers behind so I want them to read this book and start living.

2. Coming across the Red Pill community. I realized that the secular form of the Red Pill will help men a lot, and a lot of young Catholic men are going to be attracted to it – especially those raised by single moms and listening every Sunday to a lisping faggot priest who preaches to him about inclusion. However there is a lot of natural sin in the secular form, and this is unacceptable.

So I had to write this book and the focus had to be on Frame and other Red Pill topics. I do not intend this to be a "How To" book on being a husband and father, which would distract men from the purpose of this book. Instead I want to convey the broader message of Masculine Living, a life of Catholic Virtue.

So I've reached a compromise. I'll go over some life lessons I have on parenting, but I'm keeping this section short. Build Frame. Live life with skills and hobbies. Learn Game. Live as a man.

Here are some important lessons that will help the inexperienced first-time father:

1. Your three fold mission is to Lead, Provide, and Protect. Do not fail.

2. Infants and even toddlers take a huge toll on you and your wife. Make allowances for it. Remember Prudence.

3. In order to carry out your mission, you must maintain Frame. Working out is part of your duty.

4. Maintain masculine activities with your male buddies. Yes, you have to cut it back, even a lot, but it is important for you to keep your hobbies and interests, at least on some level.

5. Your prime directive is to get your wife and kids to heaven. The greatest threat is the online world. Keep a sharp eye out on attempts by the devil to infiltrate your family through electronic means, however make sure your kids are equipped to live in the digital world. Find the virtuous mean.

6. Lead a nightly family prayer. A 5 decade rosary, stripped of all of the adders, is ideal. However, go with an Our Father, Hail Mary, Glory Be, Guardian Angel Prayer, and Act of Contrition if you want. The important thing is to have family prayer time nightly.

7. Teach your boys to be men. Start "fighting" with your son when he is very young. I discovered the "rub you out" game, where my boy, who couldn't walk, would sit facing me, then I'd say "I'm going to rub you out", then I'd crawl over, head down, and start rubbing my hair on him. He'd squeal and grab my hair. Then I'd say, "You got me" and give the universal defeat symbol: I'd roll over on my back and hang my tongue out. This progressed over the years to massive Kung Fu fights such that my wife would go running out of the room when we got going.

Also, teach him sports. Get a tennis ball and start rolling it to him. Praise him when he throws it back to you, or rolls it. Teach your sons to be men.

8. Institute "Yes sir / No sir" and "Yes mam / No mam". Make sure your kids respect their mama.

9. Make sure the kids have chores. Make sure your daughters are helping their mama out and learning to run a house. This can start at around 7. Remember that little girls LOVE helping their mama with baking.

10. Get your kids into sports and activities. County programs are excellent. For boys there is baseball, wrestling, and football. For girls the go-to is classical ballet.

11. Enforce modest dress in your wife and daughters. I have no problem with pants, especially jeans, but that is your call.

12. Avoid the "bunker Trad" mindset. I don't know how many kids have been lost, who on turning 18 announce everyone is crazy and lose the Faith. You have to give your kids a social life, especially teens, and especially with the opposite sex. I love taking teens to swing dancing, because it is open to all ages, which means your kids won't feel like you are the gestapo when you chaperone (and dance with your wife). There's also Catholic teen youth groups, the March for Life, and I also recommend you arrange a trip to the Clear Creek Monastery work day in Eastern Oklahoma. It would be a fun trip and they provide camp sites, facilities, and food on the work day. Make sure that your teens are active, and can learn how to interact with the opposite sex in a moral atmosphere.

13. Lead. Plan outings and vacations. As I've mentioned earlier, don't over-complicate it. Take the little kids on a hike to go look for pine cones.

14. Discipline. Your wife's big Mommy Heart is not cut out for discipline, so you have to help her. It starts with "No!" at a

very young age. Of special note, it is your responsibility to take care of unruly kids during Mass. Take junior out to the cry room or lobby if he is crying. Don't let him play – hold him. Tell him when he is ready to be a big boy, you'll take him back to Mommy. When he settles down, ask him if he is ready to be a big boy. When he nods yes, tell him he'll come right back here if he acts up again. If he's really bad, give him a spank. He'll learn relatively quickly. Also, on spanking, never ever hit a kid in anger. Settle down first and pop him on the back of the upper leg.

15. Can your wife breast feed in Church? Yes, in Trad chapels it is generally acceptable. The mothers will cover the baby during feeding with a blanket for modesty purposes. It's not a big deal.

16. Watch your kids' diets. Avoid sugar. Make sure they are getting plenty of meat, fat, vegetables, and some fruit. A little dessert is ok, but don't let them bloat up into whales. Sugary drinks are the big problem.

17. You will likely have to homeschool. Do the research. There are now even online programs to make things a lot easier. Use a local community college for high schoolers and make sure your sons take Calculus their senior year, if they have an aptitude for that. Computer literacy and even some coding is also a must.

18. Watch your finances and budget. This comes under Provide.

19. On confession, have a policy of asking ZERO questions. If your kids skip communion, that is their business alone. If they want to go to confession, take them. Do not put any impediments in the way of them going to confession.

20. Finally, and perhaps not that important, I used a zero drinking age policy. My son probably has a beer bottle in his bedroom. Perhaps he decided a beer would taste really good at a certain point. That's fine. I have found that this has carried over to my adult children who are not mystified by alcohol, and it has never been a problem for them. I recommend this policy.

That's it for my points. I could go on and on (don't use a pacifier, use diaper cream after every changing, etc… etc…), however I've already provided some important information to keep you out of trouble.

Afterwords and Acknowledgments

And so you've reached the end. That's it, that's the Catholic Red Pill. This book, along with a few other books and online communities is the only place you will get this information. For the rest of the time you will be under the constant demoralization campaign to turn you into a simp and a cuck. What this means is that you have to read this book cover-to-cover at least three times. The sections where you need the most improvement will stand out and this will help you to improve quickly. Beyond that I recommend reviewing the book weekly to monthly, especially going over Frame to keep you from slipping.

I also am very cognizant that I have given you the ideal. You will fall short, but hopefully you'll come closer than I have – you have the book. Do not let this book get you down, especially if you are starting out in a deep hole. No. This book is hope. You now have knowledge, so take the next step. Start improving. This is a life long process, so give yourself a few months until you start checking for results. Consider this: a lot of this material was derived from my screw ups. I learned about women by making a fool of myself in High School. So don't get discouraged, develop Frame and live life.

I'd like to list some acknowledgments. Most are heathens, and in this day-and-age of speed-of-light information, I'm not even sure if they are the originators. You can assume I've used a lot of other people's work, but a lot includes my interpretations, or even my original content. If some part seems familiar to you, chances are I shamelessly stole it.

Aaron Clary. America's Favorite Heathen and Misanthrope. I borrowed heavily from him on education. If there is a chance of one of these men converting, it will be Aaron. Say a prayer for his conversion.

Corey Wayne. Dating Coach. I haven't dated a single woman in 28 years, so I relied heavily on him.

Rollo Tomassi. One of the original moderators of So Suave and one of the fathers of Red Pill. He's a secularist. I listened to some of his stuff for general knowledge.

Rich Cooper. He is a big proponent of being the best version of yourself. I used some of his concepts in the book.

Vox Day. Heavily involved with Gamer Gate and an expert on the history of the Alt Right. The only Christian in the bunch.

I also want to thank Mary Jo and Jimencio Arte for the great cover. If you didn't catch it, those are redpills on the tray.

One final thing lads, ask yourself: all along are we gaming the women, or have they been gaming us? It's all fun so enjoy life.

Made in the USA
Columbia, SC
29 July 2021